CAMBRIDGE NATIONAL LEVEL 1/LEVEL 2

Engineering Manufacture

Revision Guide and Workbook

Paul Anderson and Andrew Buckenham

CAMBRIDGE
UNIVERSITY PRESS

Shaftesbury Road, Cambridge CB2 8EA, United Kingdom

One Liberty Plaza, 20th Floor, New York, NY 10006, USA

477 Williamstown Road, Port Melbourne, VIC 3207, Australia

314–321, 3rd Floor, Plot 3, Splendor Forum, Jasola District Centre, New Delhi – 110025, India

103 Penang Road, #05–06/07, Visioncrest Commercial, Singapore 238467

Cambridge University Press & Assessment is part of the University of Cambridge.

It furthers the University's mission by disseminating knowledge in the pursuit of education, learning and research at the highest international levels of excellence.

www.cambridge.org
Information on this title: www.cambridge.org/9781009121910

© Cambridge University Press & Assessment 2022

This publication is in copyright. Subject to statutory exception and to the provisions of relevant collective licensing agreements, no reproduction of any part may take place without the written permission of Cambridge University Press & Assessment.

First published 2022

20 19 18 17 16 15 14 13 12 11 10 9 8 7 6 5 4 3

Printed in Great Britain by CPI Group (UK) Ltd, Croydon CR0 4YY

A catalogue record for this publication is available from the British Library

ISBN   978-1-009-12191-0   Paperback with Digital Access (1 Year)
ISBN   978-1-009-11392-2   Digital Learner's Book (1 Year)

Additional resources for this publication at www.cambridge.org/9781009121910

Cambridge University Press & Assessment has no responsibility for the persistence or accuracy of URLs for external or third-party internet websites referred to in this publication, and does not guarantee that any content on such websites is, or will remain, accurate or appropriate. Information regarding prices, travel timetables, and other factual information given in this work is correct at the time of first printing but Cambridge University Press & Assessment does not guarantee the accuracy of such information thereafter.

....

NOTICE TO TEACHERS IN THE UK
It is illegal to reproduce any part of this work in material form (including photocopying and electronic storage) except under the following circumstances:
(i) where you are abiding by a licence granted to your school or institution by the Copyright Licensing Agency;
(ii) where no such licence exists, or where you wish to exceed the terms of a licence, and you have gained the written permission of Cambridge University Press & Assessment;
(iii) where you are allowed to reproduce without permission under the provisions of Chapter 3 of the Copyright, Designs and Patents Act 1988, which covers, for example, the reproduction of short passages within certain types of educational anthology and reproduction for the purposes of setting examination questions.

....

Contents

Preparing for the exam

Your Revision Guide and Workbook	4
Planning your revision	5
Revision techniques	7
Getting ready for the exam	9
What to expect in the exam	10
Revision checklist	16

Unit R014: Principles of engineering manufacture

Revision Guide

TA1:	Manufacturing processes	18
TA2:	Engineering materials	45
TA3:	Manufacturing requirements	55
TA4:	Developments in engineering manufacture	62

Workbook

TA1:	Manufacturing processes	67
TA2:	Engineering materials	85
TA3:	Manufacturing requirements	94
TA4:	Developments in engineering manufacture	102

Glossary

Key terms	109
Command words	110

Answers

Answers to 'Practise it!' activities	112
Answers to Workbook questions	114

Acknowledgements 126

Preparing for the exam

Your Revision Guide and Workbook

This Revision Guide will support you in preparing for the exam for Unit R014 Principles of engineering manufacture. This is the externally assessed unit of your Engineering Manufacture J823 course.

The Revision Guide contains two types of pages, as shown below:

- content pages to help you revise the content you need to know.
- workbook pages with practice exam-style questions to help you prepare for your exam.

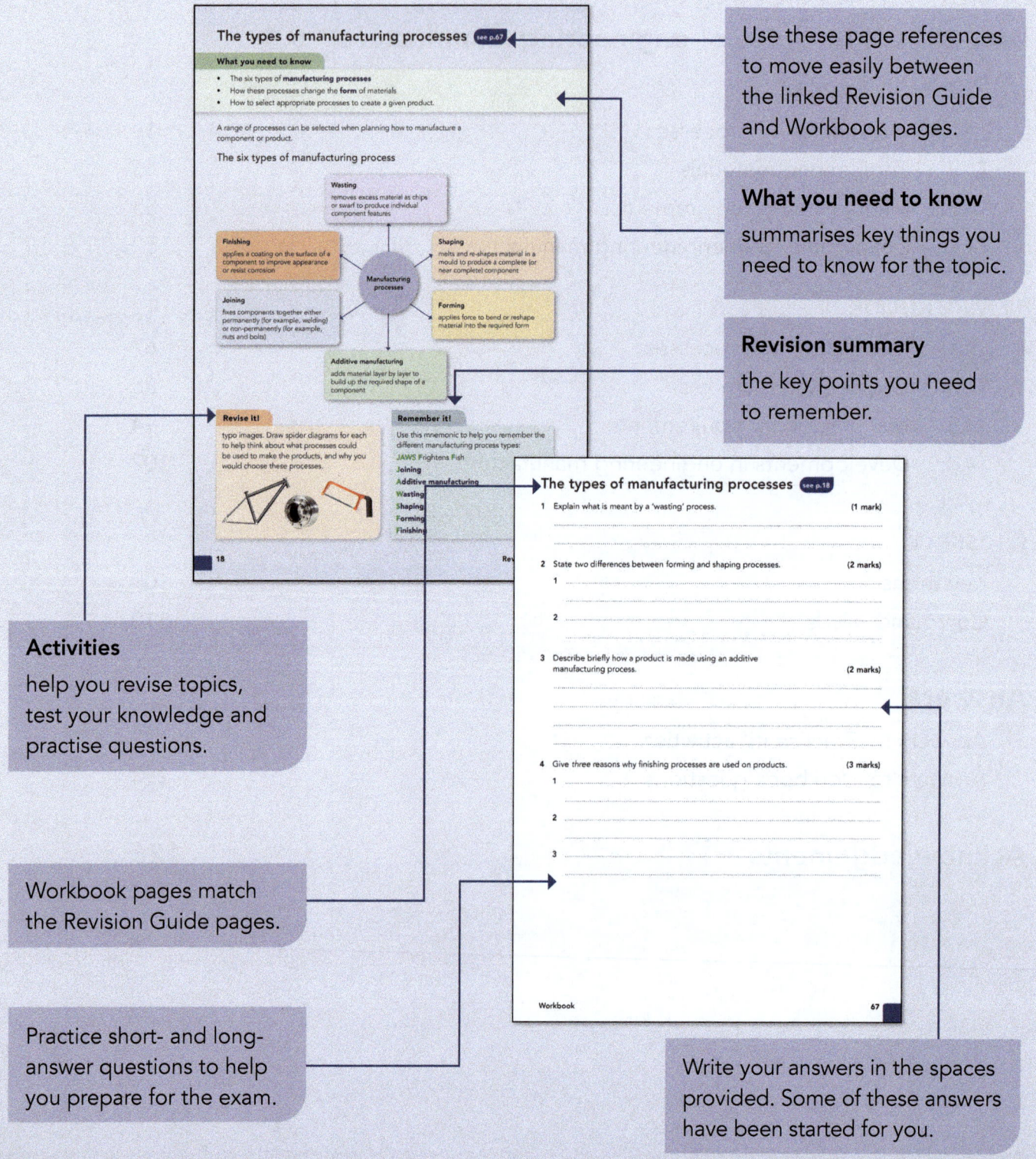

Use these page references to move easily between the linked Revision Guide and Workbook pages.

What you need to know summarises key things you need to know for the topic.

Revision summary the key points you need to remember.

Activities help you revise topics, test your knowledge and practise questions.

Workbook pages match the Revision Guide pages.

Practice short- and long-answer questions to help you prepare for the exam.

Write your answers in the spaces provided. Some of these answers have been started for you.

4   Preparing for the exam

Planning your revision

Countdown to the exam

Revision checklists are a good way for you to plan and structure your revision.
They also allow you to make sure you have covered everything you need to cover.

Revision planner checklist

Time before the exam	Things to do	
6–8 weeks	• Draw up a revision timetable so that you know how much time you have to get through everything.	☐
	• Use the revision checklist on page 16 to work out which topics you need to cover.	☐
	• Use the topic area headings and bullets to organise your notes and to make sure you've covered everything in the specification.	☐
	• Don't do too much in one day – a couple of hours of good-quality work in a day is better than trying to cram.	☐
4–6 weeks	• Work out which of the areas you still find difficult and plan when you'll cover them.	☐
	• You may be able to discuss tricky topics with your teacher or class colleagues.	☐
	• As you feel you've got to grips with some of the knowledge, you can 'tick off' the parts that have been worrying you.	☐
	• Make the most of the revision sessions you're offered in class. Don't skip them!	☐
1 week	• Make a daily plan to revise those few topics you're not happy with and look back at your revision cards (see page 7) if you've made some.	☐
Day before	• Try not to cram today – get some exercise and relax in the afternoon.	☐
	• Make sure you know what time and where the exam is and put all your things out (pencils, pens, calculator, bus pass, water) ready for the next day.	☐
	• Get a good night's sleep!	☐

> **Revise it!**
>
> Using the example above, create your own revision checklist. Identify areas that you are not so confident about and think of ways to tackle these.

Preparing for the exam

Revision tips

Choose the methods that work for you

For example:
- use highlighters for key words and phrases
- make note cards
- use mnemonics (the first letter of words): for example, **J**AWS **F**rightens **F**ish stands for **J**oining, **A**dditive manufacturing, **W**asting, **S**haping, **F**orming, **F**inishing.

Plan your revision

Make a list of all the key dates from when you start your revision up to the exam date.

Take breaks

Plan regular breaks in your revision. Go for a short walk or get some fresh air. It will make you more focused when you do revise!

Learn everything!

Questions can be asked about **any area** of the specification.

It is easier to answer a question if you have revised everything.

Don't cram!

Plan to space your revision out so that you don't do everything at once!

Use mind maps!

Mind maps are great for connecting ideas and memorising information more easily and quickly.

Identify your strengths and weaknesses

Complete the 'Revision checklist' at the end of each chapter and identify areas that you feel less confident about. Allow additional time to revise these areas.

Stay healthy!

Exercise, fresh air, good food and staying hydrated all help your revision.

Attend revision classes!

Don't skip revision classes – it can really help to revise with your friends as well as by yourself.

Practise!

Practising exam-style questions will help you get to grips with the question types, time pressure and format of the exam.

Variety is the spice of life!

Mix up your revision methods. Watch videos and listen to podcasts as well as making notes and mind maps.

Find a quiet space

It can be difficult to revise in loud or busy spaces, so try to find somewhere calm to work. You could use headphones and music to block out distractions.

Revision techniques

Flash cards/revision cards

These are useful for summarising content, key word definitions and important facts. Use colours to make certain things stand out, for example, you could use different colours for advantages and disadvantages or for key words. You can test yourself using the revision cards.

Mind maps

These are a really useful visual summary of information and you can put them on the wall. They allow you to show links between ideas and concepts. You can start by adding the topic to the centre of the diagram and then add the sub-topics around that and a summary of the information.

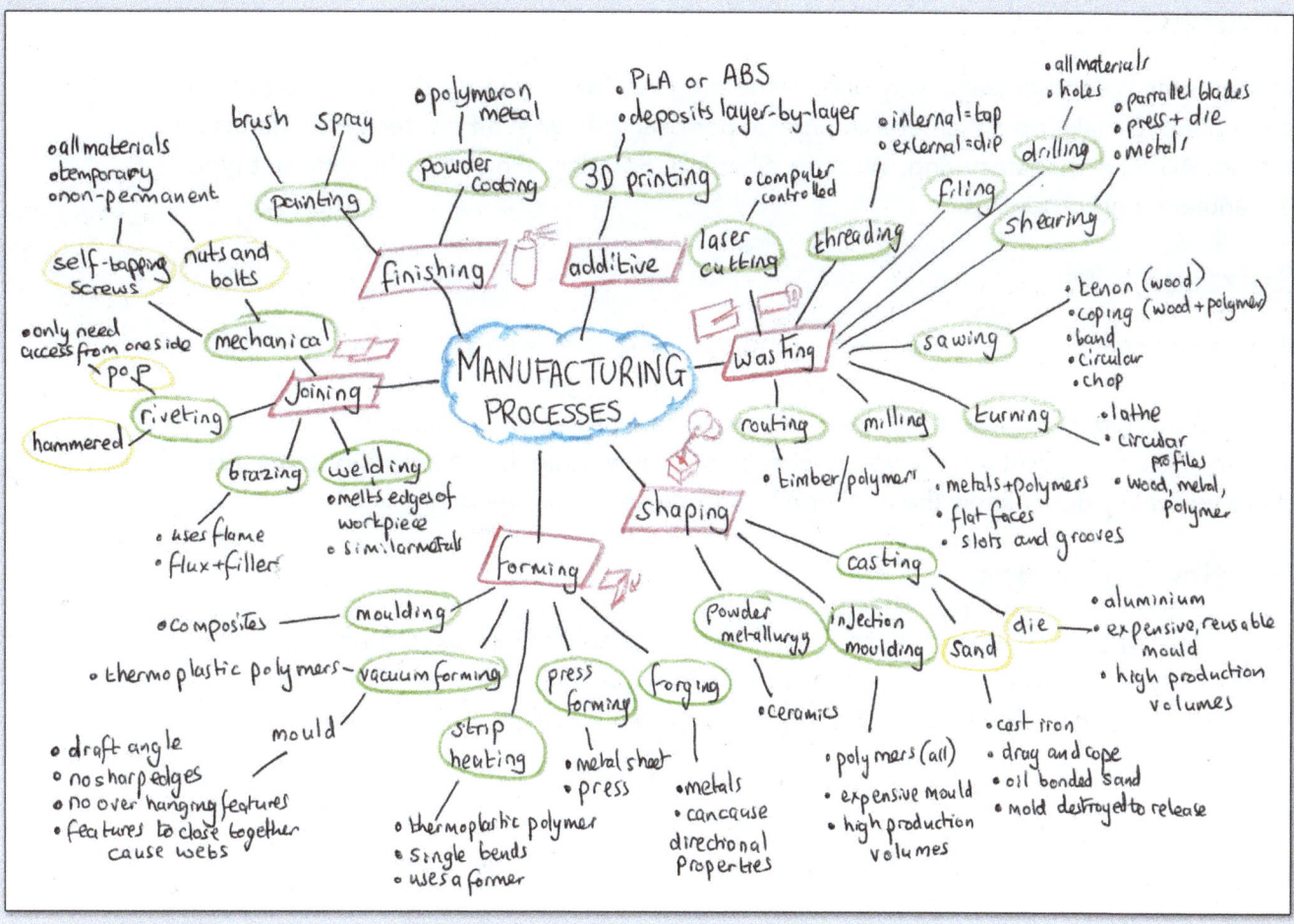

Revise it!

Create a mind map for a topic of your choice.

Preparing for the exam

Highlighting

Making notes and highlighting key areas to go back to is a good way of working out what you know and don't know. You can then use these notes as you come to your final revision. You can use different colours to highlight different factors or different types of information. For example, when revising metals as a material, you could colour-code metals that are ferrous and metals that are non-ferrous.

Summaries

On the revision pages of this book, you'll find summaries of key ideas and themes. Use these to help you summarise the key points you'll need to remember to answer questions on those topics. For example, you need to know the different types of manufacturing processes. You can make a summary of these yourself – and if you think through these points in the exam, you are more likely to remember them.

Mnemonics

A **mnemonic** is another useful way of remembering key facts by using the first letter of each of the parts to make up a memorable phrase. For example, **J**AWS **F**rightens **F**ish stands for **J**oining, **A**dditive manufacturing, **W**asting, **S**haping, **F**orming, **F**inishing (the different types of manufacturing processes).

Quizzes

Many people enjoy quizzes, and creating and sharing quizzes with your friends and class is a great way to remember facts and concepts. You could suggest to your teacher that, in pairs, you create a quiz of ten questions each week and go through with another pair – swapping answers. It's also a good way for you to check your knowledge. Make a note of the areas where you really didn't know the answer and add these to your revision list.

Practice questions

Doing past papers and practice exam questions is an essential part of your revision. It prepares you for answering different types of exam questions and allows you to become familiar with the wording of the questions used by OCR.

You should also use the mark scheme. This will help you understand how to get full marks for each question.

It is helpful to highlight key words in exam questions so you're clear what the question is asking before you answer it.

Getting ready for the exam

Use the revision checklist and all your revision material to make sure you are as prepared as possible. Practise plenty of exam questions and quick quizzes.

In the exam
Give yourself time to complete the whole paper and check through it for mistakes. Most importantly, try to stay calm and relaxed – remember, this is your time to show off what you know!

Get plenty of sleep
Make sure you get a good night's sleep the night before the exam. Don't stay up late cramming as you need time to switch off and relax before going to bed.

Keep hydrated but don't drink too much
It's important that you stay hydrated but don't overdo it or you'll be running to the toilet. Exams can make you a bit nervous too which means you might need to go to the toilet a bit more frequently. Water is best.

Eat a good, healthy meal
Have a good healthy meal that you enjoy the night before the exam and a filling breakfast on the day of the exam to give you a boost ready for your exam.

Make sure you have all the things you need
Get everything ready the night before – including all writing equipment, a calculator if you need one (and are allowed one), a water bottle, tissues and any identification you might need (candidate number if you have been given one).

Set your alarm
If your exam is in the morning, set an alarm or **two** so you have plenty of time to get to the exam. If you're still worried about oversleeping, ask a friend or someone in your family to make sure you're up.

Arrive in plenty of time
Know when and where the exam is. Get there at least 15 minutes before it starts. If your exam is in an unfamiliar part of the school and away from where you normally study, you might have to leave home a bit earlier. Don't be distracted on the way!

Don't be tempted to do too much cramming
Too much last-minute cramming can scramble your brain! You may find that being relaxed will help you recall the facts you need rather than attempting last-minute cramming, but you may also want to revise the key facts before setting off for the exam.

Getting ready for the exam

Preparing for the exam

What to expect in the exam

As part of your qualification in Engineering Manufacture you will be taking an exam that is worth 70 marks. It is important that from the beginning you start to think about the exam and the skills you'll need to get the best possible grade. Answering exam questions is a skill. Like any other skill, it can be learnt, practised and improved.

Below is an outline of what to expect in the exam, the types of questions and what the paper looks like. You need to answer **all** the questions.

Types of questions to expect in the exam

Exam questions can be asked about any area of the specification, which means that you have to learn everything!

The exam paper will contain three types of question.

Question type	Description
Multiple-choice question (MCQ)	• A question with four answer options. • Worth 1 mark.
Short answer question	• Usually require a one-word answer or a simple sentence. • Worth 1–4 marks.
Long answer question	• Open response question where you are expected to do a piece of extended writing. • Worth up to 6 marks.

These questions allow you to be assessed on the quality of your written communication.

Understanding the language of the exam

The command word is the key term that tells you how to answer the question. It is essential to know what the different command words mean and what they are asking you to do. It is easy to confuse the words and provide too much information, not enough information or the wrong information. The tables below will help you understand what each command word is asking you to do.

Command words that ask you to get creative

Command word	OCR definition	How you should approach it
Create	• Produce a visual solution to a problem (for example, a mind map, flow chart or visualisation).	Show your answer in a visual way. You might want to use a mind map, flow chart or a diagram. Think about what is the best way to show the required information.
Draw	• Produce a picture or diagram.	Create a picture/diagram to show the relevant information.

Command words that ask you to do your maths

Command word	OCR definition	How you should approach it
Calculate	• Get a numerical answer showing how it has been worked out.	Do your maths. Give the final answer but make sure you show how you got there.

Command words that ask you to choose the correct answer

Command word	OCR definition	How you should approach it
Choose	• Select an answer from options given.	Pick the option that you think is correct.
Circle	• Select an answer from options given.	Draw a circle around the correct answer.
Identify	• Select an answer from options given. • Recognise, name or provide factors or features.	Either choose the correct answer from those given or write the name, factors or features that are asked for.

Command words that ask you to add to something

Command word	OCR definition	How you should approach it
Annotate	• Add information, for example, to a table, diagram or graph until it is final. • Add all the needed or appropriate parts.	Add short notes to the table/diagram/graph to say what each part is.
Complete	• Add all the needed or appropriate parts. • Add information, for example, to a table, diagram or graph until it is final.	Add the information that is missing. Often you will need to give just one word as an answer but sometimes you may need to write more. You may need to finish drawing a diagram or graph.
Fill in	• Add all the needed or appropriate parts. • Add information, for example, to a table, diagram or graph until it is final.	Add the information that is missing. Often you will need to give just one word as an answer but sometimes you may need to write more.
Label	• Add information, for example, to a table, diagram or graph until it is final. • Add all the necessary or appropriate parts.	This often refers to a diagram or a picture. Add words or short phrases to say what each part is. You could add arrows next to your label that point to the right part of the diagram/graph.

Command words that ask you to give the main points

Command word	OCR definition	How you should approach it
Outline	• Give a short account, summary or description.	Write about the main points. Don't write lots of detailed information.
State	• Give factors or features. • Give short, factual answers.	Give a short answer that names factors or features of something. Sometimes you will be asked to give a certain number of factors/features.

Command words that ask you to be factual

Command word	OCR definition	How you should approach it
Describe	• Give an account including all the relevant characteristics, qualities or events. • Give a detailed account of.	This is the 'what'. Write about **what** something is.
Explain	• Give reasons for and/or causes of. • Use the words or phrases such as 'because', 'therefore' or 'this means that' in answers.	This is the '**how**' and the '**why**'. Write about how something happens or works and why it does.

Preparing for the exam

Command words that ask you to give an opinion

Command word	OCR definition	How you should approach it
Analyse	• Separate or break down information into parts and identify its characteristics or elements. • Explain the pros and cons of a topic or argument and make reasoned comments. • Explain the impacts of actions using a logical chain of reasoning.	This term wants you to write about the details. Write about each part in turn, giving key information and saying what is good or bad about it.
Compare and contrast	• Give an account of the similarities and differences between two or more items or situations.	'Compare' means to say what is the **same** about two (or more) things. 'Contrast' means to say what is **different** about two (or more) things.
Discuss	• Present, analyse and evaluate relevant points (for example, for/against an argument).	Write about something in detail, including its strengths and weaknesses. Say what you think about each side of the argument. You don't need to take a side.
Evaluate	• Make a reasoned qualitative judgement considering different factors and using available knowledge/experience.	Write down the arguments for and against something. Then give your opinion about which is the strongest argument.
Justify	• Give good reasons for offering an opinion or reaching a conclusion.	Write what you think would be the best option and say why you think this. Give evidence to support your answer.

> **Practise it!**
>
> Now go to www.cambridge.org/go and complete the practice questions on understanding the exam command words.

Common exam mistakes

Common mistakes	Why it matters!	Solutions
Not attempting a question	You won't get any marks for a blank answer	• Answer every question. • Write something – you may pick up a few marks, which can add up to make the difference between grades. • Use your general knowledge. • State the obvious. • Think, 'What would my teacher say to that?'
Not answering the question that is asked	You won't get any marks for writing about another topic or for answering the wrong command word.	• Know what the command words are looking for. • RTQ – read the question. • ATQ – answer the question.
Not providing enough points to achieve the marks	You won't gain full marks if you haven't expanded on your answer.	• Look at the number of marks next to the question – 1 mark = 1 point; 2 marks = 2 points, 3 marks = 3 points, etc. • Consider if the question requires further explanation or discussion.

Answering long-answer questions

Planning your answer

To help you organise your thoughts, it is helpful to plan your answer for 6-mark questions. You don't need to take too long. A spider diagram, for example, will help you get your answer in the right order and it makes sure you don't forget anything. For example:

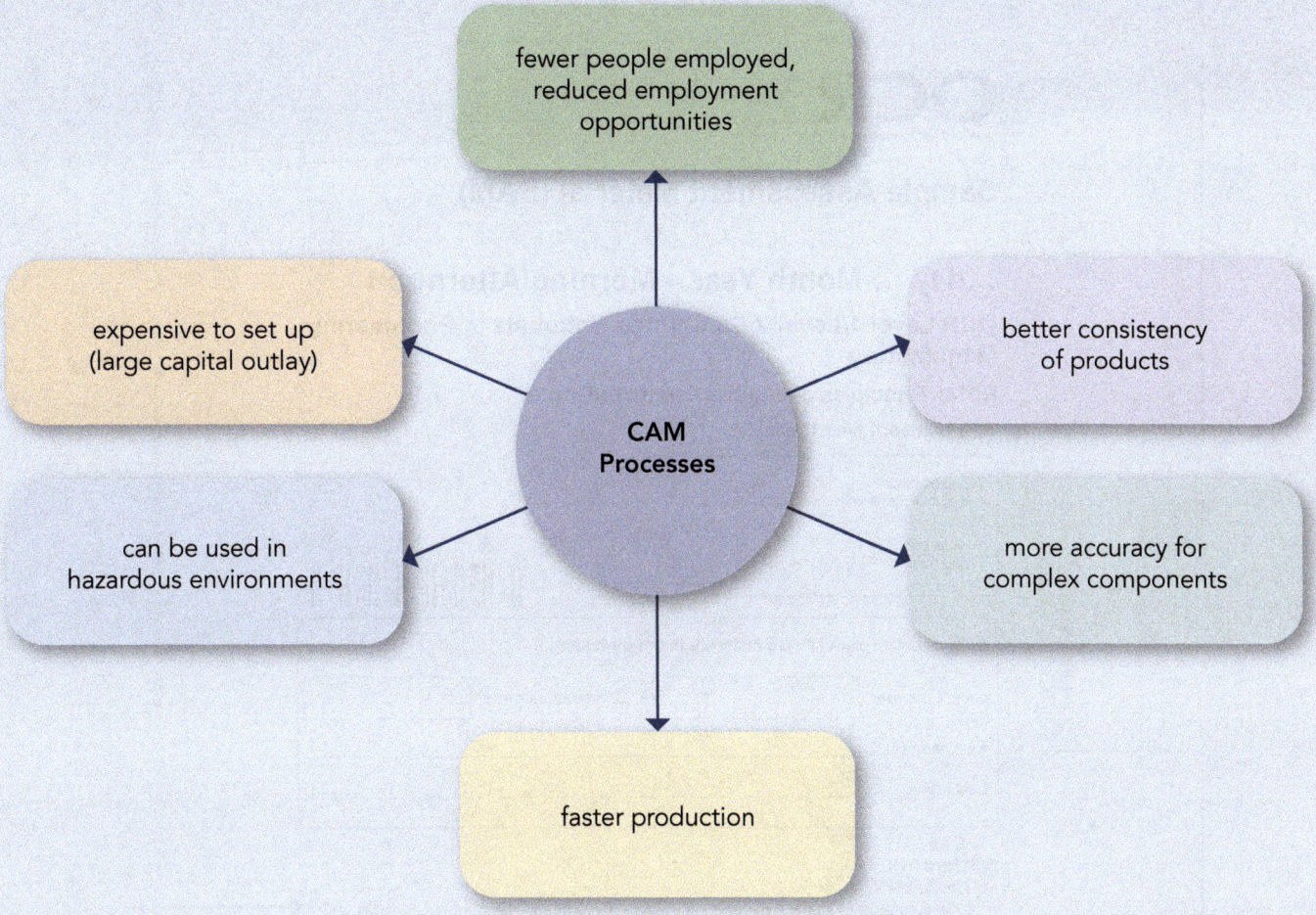

Revise it!

Create a spider diagram plan like the one above for the following question:
Describe how you would manufacture a component using vacuum forming.

Tip: You could refer to page 36 of the Revision Guide to help you.

Preparing for the exam

The exam paper

Make sure you know how long you have got.

Write your first name and surname clearly in the boxes.

Ensure that you write clear, structured answers so that you can get maximum marks.

OCR
Oxford Cambridge and RSA

Sample Assessment Material (SAM)

…day … Month Year – Morning/Afternoon

OCR Level 1/Level 2 Cambridge Nationals in Engineering Manufacture

R014: Principles of engineering manufacture

Time allowed: 1 hour 15 minutes

You must have:
- No extra materials are needed

You can use:
- A calculator

Write clearly in black ink. **Do not write in the barcodes.**

Centre number ☐☐☐☐☐ Candidate number ☐☐☐☐

First name(s) _____

Last name _____

INSTRUCTIONS
- Use black ink.
- Write your answer to each question in the space provided. You can use extra paper if you need to, but you must clearly show your candidate number, the centre number and the question numbers.
- Answer **all** the questions.

INFORMATION
- The total mark for this paper is **70**.
- The marks for each question are shown in brackets **[ ]**.
- This document has **16** pages.

ADVICE
- Read each question carefully before you start your answer.

© OCR 2021 […/…/…]
DC (…) 000000
Version 2 (July 2021)

OCR is an exempt Charity

Turn over

---

14 — Preparing for the exam

> The question is asking for two points. Be sure to give two points in your answer to get full marks.

13 (a) Explain what is meant by a smart material.

....
....
....
.... [2]

(b) Identify and explain **one** use of **each** of these smart materials.

Quantum Tunneling Composite (QTC) ....
....
....
.... [2]

Thermochromic pigment ....
....
....
.... [2]

(c) The composite material Carbon Reinforced Polymer (CRP) is used to make the frames for high performance racing bicycles.

Describe how you would make the frames from CRP.

....
....
....
....
....
....
....
.... [4]

© OCR 2021
Version 2 July 2021

> Highlight or underline key words in the question. Here you need to make specific reference to Carbon Reinforced Polymer.

> The number of marks indicates the number of points you need to give. In this case, four points are needed.

Preparing for the exam 15

Revision checklist

Topic Area	What you should know	🔴	🟠	🟢
Topic Area 1: Manufacturing Processes	**1.1 Types of manufacturing processes**			
	• The types of manufacturing processes	☐	☐	☐
	1.2 Details of different manufacturing processes			
	• Wasting processes: Sawing	☐	☐	☐
	• Wasting processes: Filing	☐	☐	☐
	• Wasting processes: Shearing	☐	☐	☐
	• Wasting processes: Drilling	☐	☐	☐
	• Wasting processes: Threading	☐	☐	☐
	• Wasting processes: Laser cutting	☐	☐	☐
	• Wasting processes: Milling/routing	☐	☐	☐
	• Wasting processes: Turning	☐	☐	☐
	• Shaping processes: Die casting	☐	☐	☐
	• Shaping processes: Sand casting	☐	☐	☐
	• Shaping processes: Sand casting versus die casting	☐	☐	☐
	• Shaping processes: Injection moulding	☐	☐	☐
	• Shaping processes: Powder metallurgy	☐	☐	☐
	• Forming processes: Forging	☐	☐	☐
	• Forming processes: Press forming	☐	☐	☐
	• Forming processes: Strip heating polymers	☐	☐	☐
	• Forming processes: Vacuum forming	☐	☐	☐
	• Forming processes: Moulding of GFRP composites	☐	☐	☐
	• Forming processes: Moulding of CFRP composites	☐	☐	☐
	• Additive manufacturing: 3D printing	☐	☐	☐
	• Joining processes: Brazing	☐	☐	☐
	• Joining processes: MIG/MAG welding	☐	☐	☐
	• Joining processes: Riveting	☐	☐	☐
	• Joining processes: Mechanical fastening	☐	☐	☐
	• Finishing processes: Painting and powder coating	☐	☐	☐
Topic Area 2: Engineering materials	**2.1 Mechanical properties of materials**			
	• Strength, elasticity, ductility and hardness	☐	☐	☐
	2.2 Other properties influencing manufacturing			
	• Malleability, machinability, cost and sustainability	☐	☐	☐
	2.3 Types of engineering materials and how they are processed			
	• Metals: Ferrous metal alloys	☐	☐	☐

	• Metals: Aluminium alloys	☐	☐	☐
	• Metals: Copper, brass and bronze	☐	☐	☐
	• Polymers: Thermoplastic polymers	☐	☐	☐
	• Polymers: Thermosetting polymers	☐	☐	☐
	• Engineering ceramics	☐	☐	☐
	• Composite materials	☐	☐	☐
	• Smart materials	☐	☐	☐
Topic Area 3: Manufacturing requirements	3.1 Interpreting orthographic third angle projection drawings			
	• BS EN 8888	☐	☐	☐
	• Line types and abbreviations	☐	☐	☐
	• Dimensions, tolerances and surface finish	☐	☐	☐
	• Mechanical features	☐	☐	☐
	3.2 Influence of the scale of manufacture on the production method			
	• Scales of manufacture	☐	☐	☐
	• Know the advantages and limitations of using CAM machines to manufacture parts	☐	☐	☐
	• Computer aided manufacturing (CAM)	☐	☐	☐
	3.3 Quality			
	• Quality systems	☐	☐	☐
Topic Area 4: Developments in engineering manufacture	4.1 Inventory management			
	• Material requirements planning (MRP)	☐	☐	☐
	• Just in time (JIT) manufacturing	☐	☐	☐
	4.2 Lean manufacturing			
	• Seven wastes 1: Transportation, inventory, movement	☐	☐	☐
	• Seven wastes 2: Waiting, over-processing, over production, defects	☐	☐	☐
	4.3 Globalisation			
	• Globalisation	☐	☐	☐

Revision checklist

The types of manufacturing processes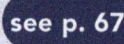

What you need to know

- The six types of **manufacturing processes**
- How these processes change the **form** of materials
- How to select appropriate processes to create a given product.

A range of processes can be selected when planning how to manufacture a component or product.

The six types of manufacturing process

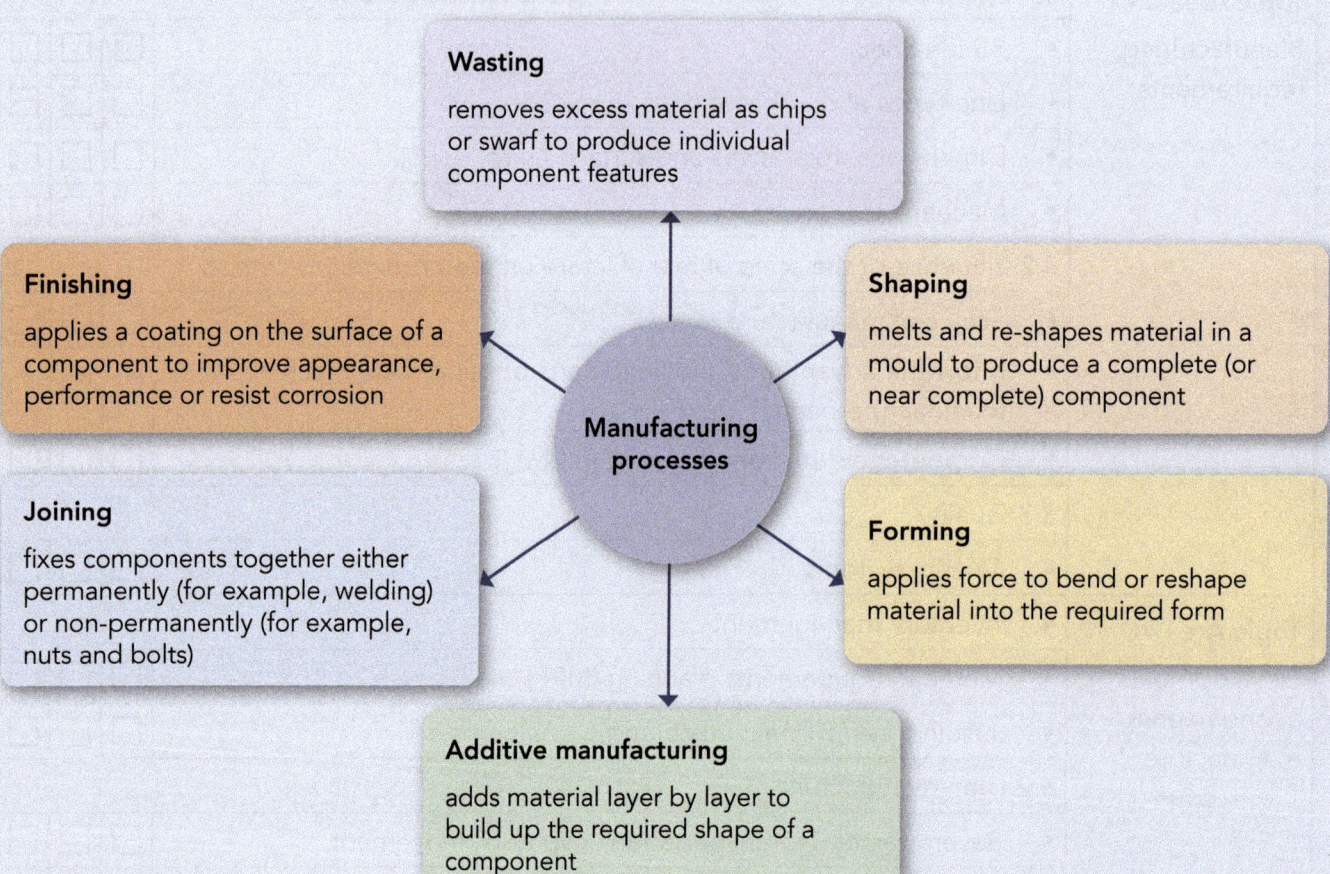

Wasting removes excess material as chips or swarf to produce individual component features

Shaping melts and re-shapes material in a mould to produce a complete (or near complete) component

Forming applies force to bend or reshape material into the required form

Additive manufacturing adds material layer by layer to build up the required shape of a component

Joining fixes components together either permanently (for example, welding) or non-permanently (for example, nuts and bolts)

Finishing applies a coating on the surface of a component to improve appearance, performance or resist corrosion

Revise it!

Look at these images, and the hacksaw on page 19. Draw spider diagrams for each to help think about what processes could be used to make the products, and why you would choose these processes.

Remember it!

Use this mnemonic to help you remember the different manufacturing process types:

JAWS **F**rightens **F**ish
Joining
Additive manufacturing
Wasting
Shaping
Forming
Finishing

18   Revision Guide

Wasting processes: Sawing (see p. 68)

What you need to know

- The tools, equipment, steps and safety measures used when sawing.

Sawing is a wasting process that uses a thin, toothed blade to remove material and cut a narrow slit.

Types of saw

Hand tools: Hacksaw, junior hacksaw, coping saw

Power tools: Mechanical power hacksaw, band saw

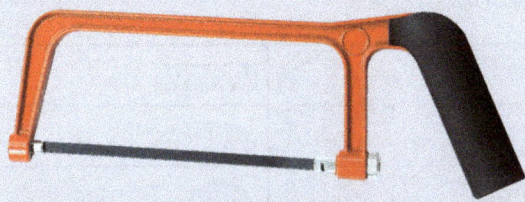

Hacksaws are used for cutting metals and polymer materials by hand.

Safe use of saws

Hand tool	Use	Safety
Hacksaw	Straight cuts in metal <30 **mm** (millimetres) thick.	Handle sharp tools with care. Do not apply excessive pressure when cutting, or blades might break. Store tools safely when not in use. Beware of burrs and sharp edges that can cause cuts.
Junior hacksaw	Straight cuts in metals and polymers <10 mm thick.	
Coping saw	Complex curved shapes in wood or polymer sheets <5 mm thick.	

Power tool	Use	Safety
Mechanical power hacksaw	Straight cuts in metal >30 mm thick.	Use only when trained in the safe operation of the equipment. Wear eye protection and substantial footwear. Secure long hair and loose clothing, and remove rings and jewellery. Ensure workpieces are clamped and/or supported appropriately. It is recommended that Band saws are not used by under-16s in schools.
Band saw	Straight or curved cuts in a wide range of materials depending on the type of blade and cutting speed used.	

Revise it!

Imagine you need to cut a length of 10 mm × 10 mm square bright mild steel bar. Which type of saw would you use and why?

How would you change your approach if you were asked to cut a larger mild steel bar that was 100 mm × 100 mm square?

Remember it!

- Use the right saw for the job (otherwise you might cause damage, breakage and injury).
- Mark out your work and *always* saw to a line.
- Only use power saws if you are trained to do so and comply with all safety requirements.

Revision Guide

Wasting processes: Filing (see p. 68)

What you need to know

- The tools, equipment, steps and safety measures used when filing.

Filing uses a wasting process to remove material from the surface of a metal component to refine its shape.

Types of file

Common shapes

Flat	
Half-round	
Round	

Using a file to remove material from a metal workpiece held in a bench vice.

Common file sizes (length): 6" (inch), 8", 10", 12"

Common file cuts (size of the teeth): Smooth cut (fine), second cut (medium), bastard (coarse)

Safe use of files

Shape	Use	Safety
Flat file	Flat surfaces and external curves.	Ensure file handles are secure before use (don't use a file without a handle).
Half round file	Internal curves.	Store tools safely when not in use.
Round file	Inside holes or tight internal curves.	Beware of burrs and sharp edges that can cause cuts.

Size: Use a file size appropriate to the size and shape of the workpiece.

Cut: Use coarse cut files to remove material quickly. Change to a finer cut when near the required shape/size to give a good surface finish.

Materials: Files can be used on **non-ferrous** and most **ferrous metals** as well as on hard polymer materials.

Practise it!

You have a large amount of steel to remove from the flat edge of a workpiece that is 8 mm thick and 150 mm long.

Identify the type of file that would be most appropriate to use. **(1 mark)**

a 12" flat bastard file
b 8" half round second cut file
c 12" flat smooth cut file
d 6" round file

Remember it!

- Choose the right shape, size and cut of file for the job.
- Mark out your work and *always* file to a line.

20 Revision Guide

Wasting processes: Shearing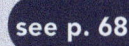

What you need to know

- The tools, equipment, steps and safety measures used when shearing.

Shearing is used to cut metal sheet material using tools and equipment that employ a shearing action. The same principle is used when scissors cut through paper.

Types of shearing tools

Hand tools: Tin snips (straight, right hand or left hand)

Manually operated machinery:
Foot operated manual guillotine

The image shows a pair of tin snips being used to cut thin sheet metal.

Safe use of shearing tools and equipment

Tool	Use	Safety
Tin snips (straight)	Straight cuts in sheet metal (typically 0.8 mm maximum sheet thickness in mild steel).	Use appropriate manual handling techniques when moving metal sheets.
Tin snips (right hand)	Right-handed curved cuts in sheet metal (typically 0.8 mm maximum sheet thickness).	Beware of sharp points, burrs and sharp edges that can cause cuts.
Tin snips (left hand)	Left-handed curved cuts in sheet metal (typically 0.8 mm maximum sheet thickness).	Wear eye protection and substantial footwear.
Foot operated manual guillotine	Straight cuts in sheet metal (typically 1.6 mm maximum sheet thickness in mild steel). Allows long cuts to be made in a single action (typically 1300 mm maximum length).	Ensure all guards are in place prior to use. Use appropriate manual handling techniques when moving metal sheets. Beware of sharp points, burrs and sharp edges that can cause cuts. Use only when trained in the safe operation of the equipment. Wear eye protection and substantial footwear. Secure long hair and loose clothing, and remove rings and jewellery.

Practise it!

What would be the most appropriate way of making a 1200 mm straight cut in 0.6 mm thick mild steel sheet material? **(1 mark)**

a   tin snips (straight)
b   tin snips (right hand)
c   tin snips (left hand)
d   foot operated guillotine

Remember it!

- Choose the right tool for the job.
- Don't exceed the maximum material thickness.
- Wear gloves when handling metal sheets to protect you from burrs and sharp edges.

Revision Guide

Wasting processes: Drilling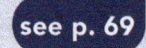

What you need to know

- The tools, equipment, steps and safety measures used when drilling.

Drilling is a very common machining operation used to produce round holes in a wide range of materials.

Types of drilling tools and equipment

Equipment: Pillar drill, portable cordless drill

Tools: Twist drills (for holes up to 13 mm diameter), hole saws (for holes larger than 13 mm diameter in sheet material)

Work holding devices: Vice, machine vice, clamps

The image shows a pillar drill being used to drill a hole in a workpiece clamped in a machine vice.

Safe use of drilling tools and equipment

Equipment	Use	Safety
Pillar drill	Used in the workshop for drilling accurately positioned, vertical holes. Speed is set according to the workpiece material and size of the drilled hole. Rotating parts are guarded. Table is adjustable to support work and allow secure work holding (using machine vice or clamps). Rotating tool is lowered vertically into the workpiece.	Use only when trained in the safe operation of the equipment. Use an appropriate speed according to the material and size of the drilled hole. Clamp the workpiece securely. Ensure all guards are in place prior to use. Wear eye protection and substantial footwear. Secure long hair and loose clothing, and remove rings and jewellery.
Portable cordless drill	Portable hand-held machine used for general drilling operations. Convenient and versatile. No guards. Single speed. Low accuracy.	

Revise it!

Draw a spider diagram to summarise drilling. Include headings such as: safety, tools, work holding and equipment.

Remember it!

- Where possible use a pillar drill as it's the safer and more accurate option.
- Use an appropriate speed according to the material and the size of the drilled hole.
- Use a series of progressively larger drill bits when drilling a large hole (maximum 13 mm diameter).
- Mark out your work and *always* centre punch the position of a hole prior to drilling.

Wasting processes: Threading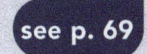

What you need to know

- The tools, equipment, steps and safety measures used when threading.

Threaded fasteners are commonly used to fix components together into assemblies.

Types of thread cutting tools

Internal thread tools:

- Taper tap
- Second cut tap   } usually supplied as a set for a given thread type and size
- Plug tap
- Tap wrench

Tap and die used in thread cutting.

Safe use of threading tools and equipment

Equipment	Use	Safety
Tap and tap wrench	Used for cutting threads on the inside of a drilled hole. Initial hole must be drilled to the correct tapping drill hole size for the thread type and size. Use thread cutting fluid to lubricate the process. Sets of taps must be used in the right order: taper, second cut and then plug.	Use correct technique and lubrication to prevent hardened steel taps from snapping or shattering in use. Wear eye protection. Avoid skin contact with swarf and thread cutting fluid. Ensure the work is held securely.
Die and die stocks	The die, which is held in a die stock, is used for cutting threads on the outside of a round metal bar. The bar must have the correct diameter for the thread size and have a small chamfer on the end before threading. Use thread cutting fluid to lubricate the process.	

Practise it!

State the correct order in which a set of three taps is used to thread hole.   **(1 mark)**

Remember it!

- Taps cut internal threads (for example, nut).
- Dies cut external threads (for example, bolt).
- Use holes and rod sizes appropriate to the threads being cut.
- Poor technique and too much force can cause taps to snap or shatter.

Revision Guide

Wasting processes: Laser cutting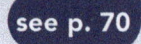

What you need to know

- The tools, equipment, steps and safety measures used when laser cutting.

Laser cutting uses a computer-controlled laser to cut complex shapes in a range of sheet materials.

Types of laser cutting tools and equipment

Computer with **computer aided design (CAD)** software; laser cutting machine; fume extraction and filtration equipment

The image shows a laser cutter being used to cut complex shapes in sheet metal.

Safe use of laser cutting equipment

Equipment	Use	Safety
CAD	Generates CAD drawing of 2D components. Exports CAD data in a format readable by the laser cutter.	Laser radiation can cause sight loss and severe burns. Use only when trained in the safe operation of the equipment. Use appropriate laser power and speed according to the material type and thickness being cut. Ensure all guards are in place prior to use. Ensure that fume extraction and filtration is used.
Laser cutting machine	Uses CAD data to control movement of the laser head and cut complex shapes from sheet materials. Laser makes cuts by causing localised extremely high temperatures that vaporise material. Laser power limits materials that can be cut (high power lasers are required to cut metals >300W).	
Fume extraction and filtration	Operation controlled automatically when the laser is in use. Extracts fumes generated when cutting. Filters out harmful particulates.	

Practise it!

State *two* advantages of using a laser cutter instead of a coping saw to cut out a **batch** of ten identical components in acrylic sheet. **(2 marks)**

Remember it!

- Laser cutting is used to cut 2D components from flat sheets.
- Component production is accurate and repeatable.
- Component design changes are quick and easy.
- Laser cutters cost between £10k and £250k.

Wasting processes: Milling/routing see pp. 69 and 70

What you need to know

- The tools, equipment, steps and safety measures used when milling/routing.

Milling and routing are similar wasting processes that use a rotating cutter to remove material from a workpiece. Milling is used primarily to machine metals and routing to cut and shape wood and manmade boards.

Types of milling/routing tools and equipment

Equipment: Vertical milling machine, portable router

Tools: End mill (face milling and slot cutting), slot drill (plunge and slot cutting), face mill (face milling used to create large, flat surfaces), routing bits (wide range available for slot cutting and edge profiling)

Work holding: Machine vice, clamps

Machining a flat surface on a workpiece using a vertical milling machine with face mill tooling.

Safe use of milling machines and routers

Equipment	Use	Safety
Milling machine	Workshop machine for accurately cutting flat surfaces and slots in metal components using a rotating tool. Rotating tool is in a fixed position. Clamped workpiece is fed into the tool by moving the machine table in X, Y and Z directions. Speed, feed and depth of cut are set according to the workpiece material, tooling and feature being machined.	Use only when trained in the safe operation of the equipment. Use appropriate operational parameters according to the material, tooling and feature being machined. Clamp the workpiece securely. Ensure all guards are in place prior to use. Wear eye protection and substantial footwear. Secure long hair and loose clothing, and remove rings and jewellery.
Router	Portable handheld machine for cutting thin material, slots and edge profiles in wood and manmade board. High speed tool rotation. Limited guarding	

Practise it!

Which of the following would be most appropriate when machining the flat mating (mounting) surface on an aluminium engine head?
- a vertical milling machine with face mill tooling
- b handheld router with profiling tool
- c vertical milling machine with end mill
- d vertical milling machine with slot drill **(1 mark)**

Remember it!

- Milling is most common in engineering applications when machining metals accurately (slot cutting and face milling).
- Routing is most common in woodworking applications (slot cutting and edge profiling).

Revision Guide   25

Wasting processes: Turning *see p. 70*

What you need to know

- The tools, equipment, steps and safety measures used when turning.

Turning is wasting process that is used to machine round bar. This might include reducing the diameter of the bar, making the ends of the bar flat and square or drilling/boring a hole along its central axis.

Types of turning tools and equipment

Equipment: Centre lathe

Tools: Facing tool (makes ends flat and square), parallel turning tool (reduces diameter), parting tool (separates finished component from bar stock), boring tool (for holes larger than 13 mm diameter), twist drill (for holes up to 13 mm diameter)

Work holding: 3-jaw lathe chuck

A centre lathe being used to turning a cylindrical component.

Turning operations: centre lathe

Use	Safety
- Workshop machine for accurately shaping a rotating metal bar using a fixed single point tool. - Turning tools are fed into the rotating workpiece by moving the tool post in the X and Y directions. - A fixed twist drill mounted in the tailstock can be used to drill a central hole in the face of the workpiece. - Speed, feed and depth of cut are set according to the workpiece material, tooling and feature being machined.	- Use only when trained in the safe operation of the equipment. - Use appropriate operational parameters according to the material, tooling and feature being machined. - Clamp the workpiece securely. - Ensure all guards are in place prior to use. - Wear eye protection and substantial footwear. - Secure long hair and loose clothing, and remove rings and jewellery.

Revise it!

Make a poster outlining the safety precautions necessary when carrying out turning operations on a centre lathe. Include appropriate illustrations of safe practice sourced online.

Remember it!

- Turning is carried out on a centre lathe.
- It is most commonly used to machine a round bar into the required shape by parallel turning, facing, drilling and boring.
- Turning in engineering applications is most often used to machine metals (although a wide range of other materials can be turned).

Shaping processes: Die casting 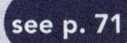 see p. 71

What you need to know

- The tools, equipment, steps and safety measures used in die casting.

Hot chamber die casting is a shaping process in which high pressure molten metal is forced into two-piece reusable hardened steel dies to make complex three-dimensional components.

Hot chamber die casting

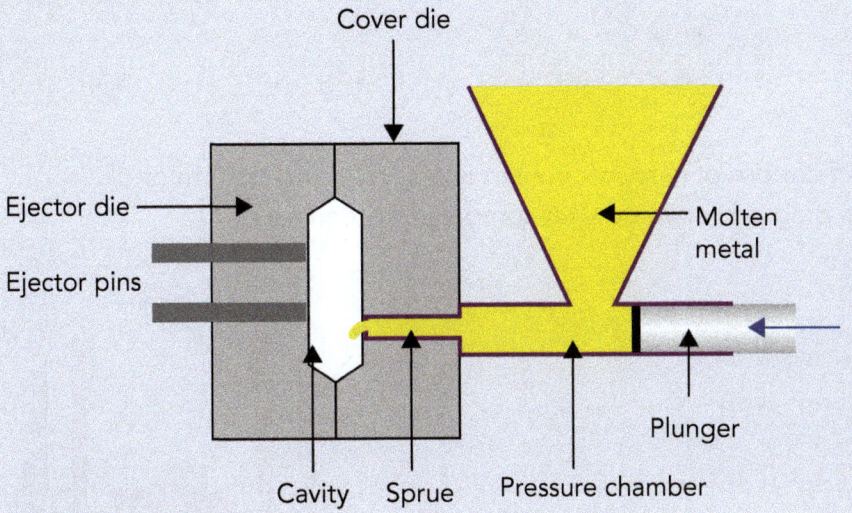

1. The two-piece metal die containing the mould cavity is held closed.
2. Molten casting metal fills the pressure chamber.
3. The plunger forces a pre-measured shot of molten metal into the die cavity.
4. The molten metal cools and the casting solidifies.
5. The two-piece die is separated.
6. Ejector pins push the casting out of the die.
7. Any remaining sprue or flash formed along the parting line is ground off the casting.
8. The two-piece metal die is closed and the cycle repeats.

Safety

Molten metal at high pressure can cause severe burns and so the whole process is enclosed during each casting cycle.

Revise it!

Draw a large sketch of the hot chamber die casting process. Add appropriate labels to identify each part using appropriate technical terms.

Remember it!

The die casting process uses a range of specific technical terms that need to be remembered. Make flashcards to match the terms with the definitions.

Mould cavity Pressure chamber Plunger
Ejector pin Sprue Parting line Flash

Revision Guide 27

Shaping processes: Sand casting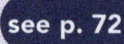

What you need to know

- The tools, equipment, steps and safety measures used in sand casting.

Sand casting is a shaping process where molten metal is poured into a green (resin bonded) expendable sand mould.

Sand casting process

1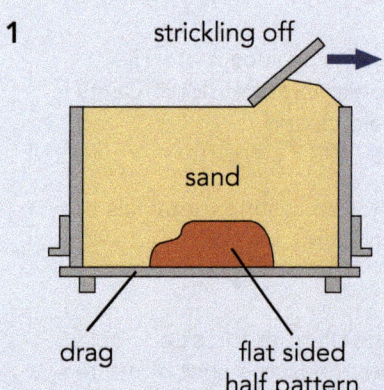

Half pattern of cast component is placed in the bottom of the drag and covered with compacted green sand.

2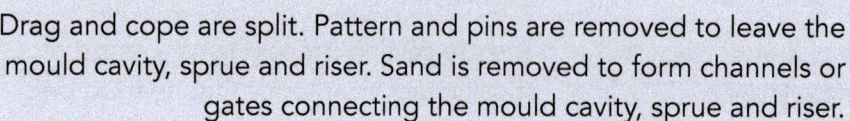

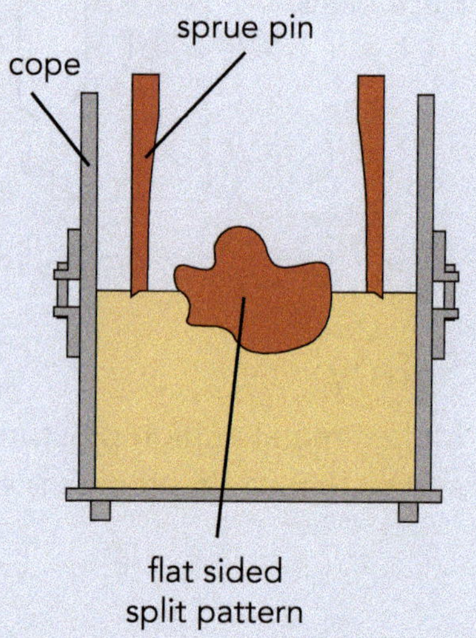

Drag is inverted and cope bolted in place. Second half of pattern and pins for sprue and riser are added.

3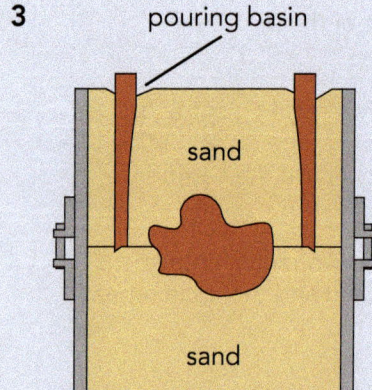

Cope is filled with compacted green sand. A pouring basin is formed around the sprue pin.

Drag and cope are split. Pattern and pins are removed to leave the mould cavity, sprue and riser. Sand is removed to form channels or gates connecting the mould cavity, sprue and riser.

4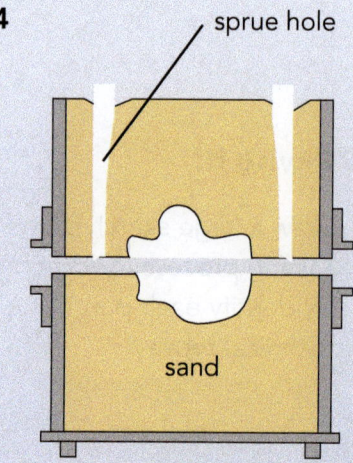

28 Revision Guide

5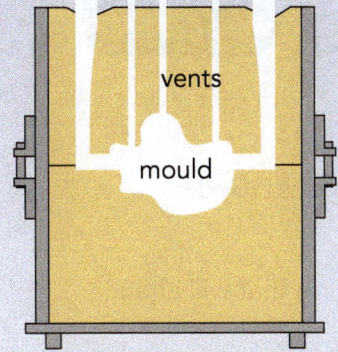

Drag and cope are securely bolted together, once the sand is fully dry. Pins are used to add vents that allow gases to escape from the mould cavity during casting.

6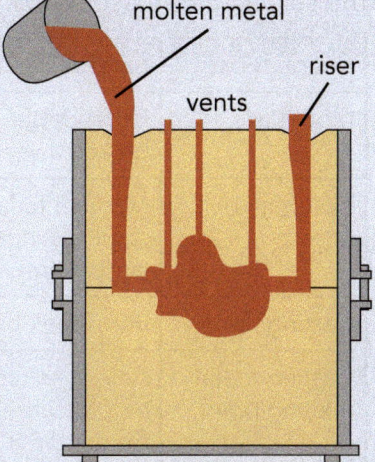

Molten metal is poured into the pouring basin and into the sprue. Pouring is stopped when molten metal emerges from the riser.

7 Once it has cooled the mould is broken off the component. Much of the green sand can be reused to make new moulds.

8 During fettling the sprues, gates, risers and any flash formed along the mould parting lines are cut or ground off.

Waste metal is recycled for use in new castings.

Safety
Sand casting is a manual process and so comprehensive PPE is required when carrying it out. This might include foundry boots, gaiters, gloves, eye protection, a leather apron and fire retardant clothing.

Revise it!
Create flashcards to help match up the unfamiliar technical terms that are used in sand casting with their definitions (see Remember it!)

Remember it!
The sand casting process uses a range of specific technical terms that need to be remembered. Make flashcards to match the terms with the definitions.

Drag   Cope   Sprue   Riser
Gate   Pouring basin   Patten

Shaping processes: Die vs. sand casting   see pp. 71–72

What you need to know

- The differences between sand and die casting, including the types of mould used.

There are several significant differences between sand casting and die casting that will affect the selection of these shaping processes for particular applications.

Characteristic	Sand casting	Die casting
Mould use	Expendable: single use sand moulds are broken away from each component.	Reusable: hardened steel dies can produce up to 100 000 castings.
Component size	Medium to large: detail can be lost on small sand castings and so it is better suited to larger components.	Small to medium: equipment and tooling cost limits the size of die cast components.
Casting metal	Iron, steel, brass, aluminium.	Brass, aluminium.
Casting metal melting point	Any: even high melting point metals can be cast because high temperatures do not affect the sand mould.	Low: high melting point metals cause damage to the steel tool.
Tooling costs	Low: a wooden pattern and green sand is usually all the tooling that is needed	High: hardened steel die cast tooling is relatively expensive depending on its size and complexity.
Tooling lead time	Low: patterns are relatively quick and easy to make.	Medium to high: machining and polishing hardened steel dies is difficult and time consuming.
Equipment costs	Low: a manual process where castings are hand poured, requiring minimal equipment.	High: a highly automated process using specialist equipment.
Dimensional accuracy	Low: require secondary machining processes to achieve high dimensional accuracy, for example, on mating surfaces.	High: no additional machining processes needed.
Surface finish	Poor: component finish is only as good as the surface of the sand mould cavity.	Very good: excellent surface finish can be achieved by polishing the mould cavity.
Batch size	Low to medium: high **labour costs** and long cycle times costs limit economic batch size.	High: low labour cost and short cycle times are ideal for large batch sizes.

Practise it!

Which of these two processes, sand casting and die casting, would be best suited to manufacturing a batch of 20 000 cast iron engine blocks? **(1 mark)**

Remember it!

When choosing processes for use in a particular application it's essential that you understand their characteristics.

Shaping processes: Injection moulding 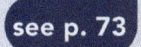 see p. 73

What you need to know

- The tools, equipment, steps and safety measures used in injection moulding.

Injection moulding is a shaping process in which high pressure molten **thermoplastic** is forced into two-piece reusable hardened steel moulds to make complex three-dimensional components.

Injection moulding process

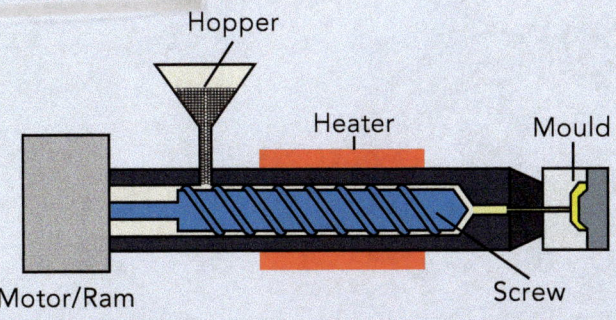

1. Thermoplastic granules are fed from a hopper into the heating chamber.
2. Granules melt as they are carried past heating elements by a rotating screw.
3. A hydraulic ram pushes the whole screw forward to force a pre-measured shot of molten thermoplastic into the mould cavity.
4. The thermoplastic cools and the moulding solidifies.
5. The mould opens and ejector pins push the finished component out.
6. Sprues and flash are removed from the components.

Process characteristics

Characteristic	Injection moulding
Mould use	Reusable: hardened steel dies can produce up to 200 000 mouldings.
Component size	Small to medium: equipment and tooling cost limits the size of injection moulded components.
Material	Thermoplastics: for example, ABS, polycarbonate.
Tooling costs	High: hardened steel moulding tools are expensive depending on size and complexity.
Tooling lead time	Medium to high: machining and polishing hardened steel dies is difficult and time consuming.
Equipment costs	High: injection moulding is a highly automated process using specialist equipment.
Dimensional accuracy	High: no additional machining processes needed.
Surface finish	Very good
Batch size	High: low labour cost and short cycle times are ideal for large batch sizes.

Safety

Molten plastic at high pressures can cause severe burns and so the whole process is enclosed during each moulding cycle.

Revise it!

Draw a series of labelled sketches to illustrate the steps involved in injection moulding.

Remember it!

Only thermoplastic materials that soften and flow when they are heated can be injection moulded.

Revision Guide

Shaping processes: Powder metallurgy 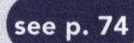 see p. 74

What you need to know

- The tools, equipment, steps and safety measures used in powder metallurgy.

Powder metallurgy is a metal forming manufacturing process that can be used as an alternative to machining, forging or casting for metallic components.

Powder metallurgy

Conventional powder metallurgy is a metal forming process that heats a compacted mix of fine metallic powders to just below their melting points. This fuses or sinters the particles of powder together into solid metallic components.

Powder metallurgy processes:

- generate very little waste
- give good surface finish
- have good dimensional accuracy
- can make porous or full density parts.

It is also possible to add non-metallic ingredients to powder metallurgy mixes. For example, tungsten carbide (an engineering ceramic) is mixed with cobalt powder and moulded into tools for use in machining.

Carbide lathe inserts are made by powder metallurgy.

Safety

The main safety issues relate to:

- high temperatures: use correct PPE and equipment (gauntlets, tongs, leather aprons)
- pressure: (enclosures, eye protection).

Conventional powder metallurgy process

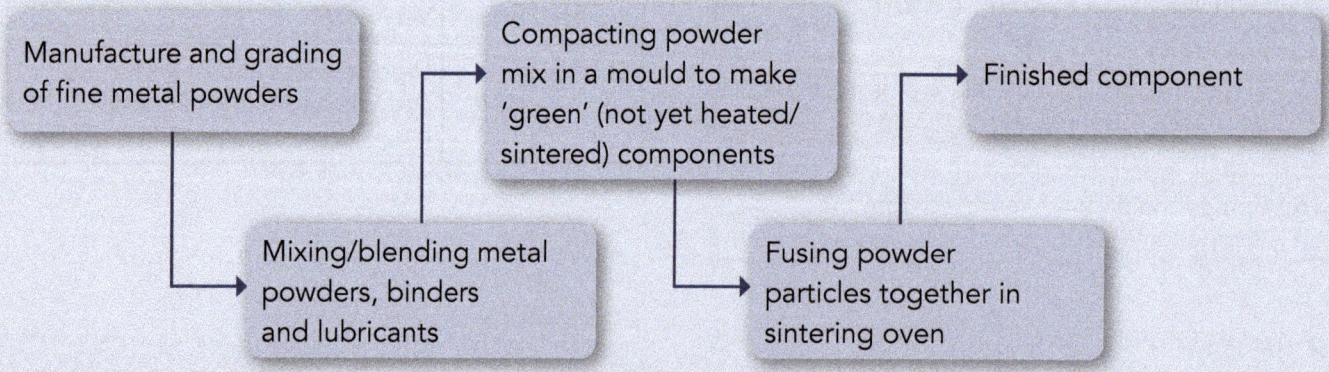

The shape of a mould needs to include a draft angle and avoid undercuts to ensure that formed components can be removed easily.

Practise it!

Explain what is meant by the term 'sintering'. **(2 marks)**

Remember it!

Powder metallurgy makes solid components by sintering together fine metal powders.

32 Revision Guide

Forming processes: Forging see p. 75

What you need to know

- The tools, equipment, steps and safety measures used in forging.

Hot forging is a forming process that uses force to reshape heated metal into a desired shape. Forged components are both stronger and tougher than equivalent cast components.

Hand forging

Blacksmiths heat steel until it becomes malleable and can be reshaped with a hammer. This type of forging has been used for centuries.

Industrial hot press forging

Press forging creates the required component shape in a single operation by taking a heated blank or billet of metal and squeezing it between shaped dies.

Excess material is squeezed out between the dies and forms a flash that must then be trimmed or ground off.

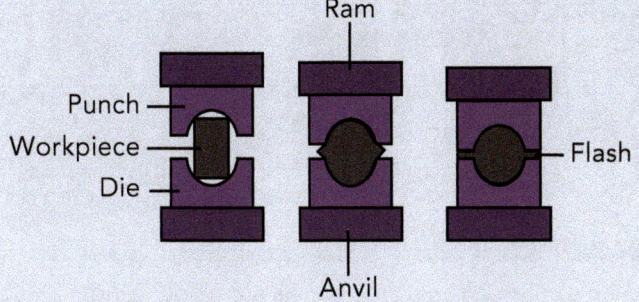

Tools and equipment

Hand forging

- Forge (coal/charcoal fire with bellows to add air reaching temperatures over 1000°C)
- Anvil
- Hand tools, for example, tongs, forging hammer, tongs, chisels, punches and drifts

Industrial hot press forging

- Flywheel or hydraulic press (able to exert hundreds or thousands of tonnes depending on the size of the component being forged)
- Forging dies (two piece hardened steel dies with a cavity in the shape of the component being forged)

Safety

Like all hot working processes, forging is potentially dangerous and appropriate PPE must always be worn, namely:

- fireproof clothing
- gauntlets
- leather apron
- safety glasses
- foundry boots
- hearing protection.

Industrial forging presses exert extremely high forces and so guards are essential to prevent trapping or impact injuries.

Revise it!

Draw a spider diagram to summarise forging. Include headings such as: safety, tooling and equipment.

Remember it!

Hot forging depends on heat to make metals malleable so they can be re-shaped.

Revision Guide

Forming processes: Press forming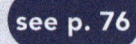

What you need to know
- The tools, equipment, steps and safety measures used in press forming metal.

Press forming is a cold forming process that bends or shapes sheet metals into components like car body panels, white goods body panels (for example, washing machines, fridges, tumble driers) or desktop computer cases.

Press forming: dedicated tooling

Complex 3D shapes such as car body panels can be formed in one operation using dedicated two-piece press tools. These are trimmed after forming.

Press forming: general purpose tooling

Sheet metal blanks can be formed into simple folded panels or boxes using a general-purpose block and blade tool on a forming press.

Complex, curved car body panels are made using dedicated press tools.

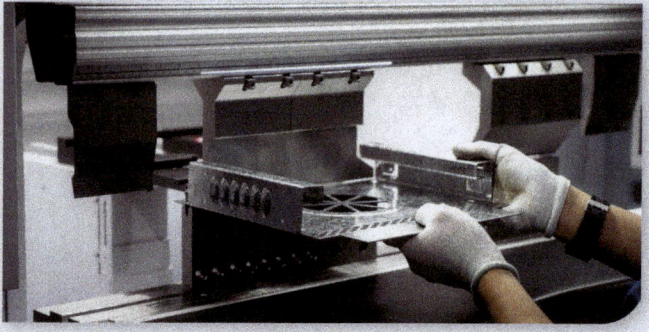

A pre-cut flat metal blank being folded into a box using a CNC press with block and blade tooling.

Tools and equipment

Large, dedicated press tools are expensive to make, can only be justified if thousands of the same component are needed and can only be used on large, powerful hydraulic presses.

General purpose block and blade tooling is much more affordable and requires a less powerful, smaller press but limits component complexity. A CNC controlled press brake with adjustable stops can form a series of folds easily and accurately.

Safety

Sheet metal has sharp edges and sharp corners and must be handled carefully.

A range of PPE should be used including:
- gloves
- safety boots
- eye protection
- hearing protection.

Presses can cause impact or crushing injuries and so machine guards must be used. These are often electronic 'light guards' that prevent the press from moving until the operator is at a safe distance.

Practise it!
Explain why dedicated press tools are only used when thousands of the same component need to be made. **(3 marks)**

Remember it!
Press forming is a cold working process to shape sheet metal components.

Forming processes: Strip heating polymers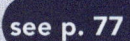

What you need to know
- The tools, equipment, steps and safety measures used in strip heating polymers.

Strip heating is a forming process for making simple components by making bends in thermoplastic sheets.

Using a strip heater

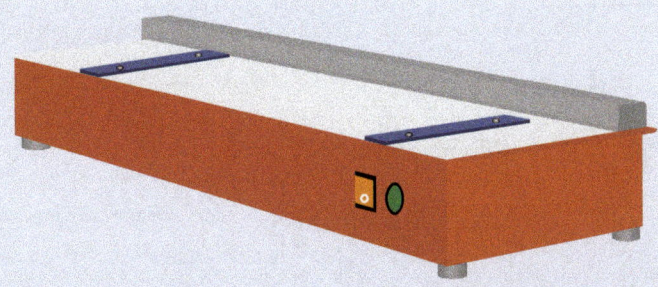

1. A flat blank (or net) of the formed component is cut out, often using a laser cutter.
2. The component is placed on the strip heater so that a fold line is directly above the heating element.
3. The strip of material along the fold line heats up and becomes pliable.
4. The component is folded to the angle required and held in position as the material cools.
5. Once fully cooled the material becomes rigid and the component holds its new shape.

Safety
- Do not touch the heating element.
- Do not touch the area of material that is being heated.
- Do not leave materials on the strip heater unsupervised.
- Allow material to cool fully before handling.

Revise it!
Create a poster that outlines the process of strip heating. Remember to include safety information.

Remember it!
- Line bending with a strip heater only works with thermoplastic sheet materials.
- Products are limited to those designed with simple straight bends.

Revision Guide 35

Forming processes: Vacuum forming (see p. 78)

What you need to know

- The tools, equipment, steps and safety measures used in vacuum forming.

Vacuum forming is used to make complex, curved, thin-walled hollow shapes from thin thermoplastic polymer sheets.

Vacuum forming

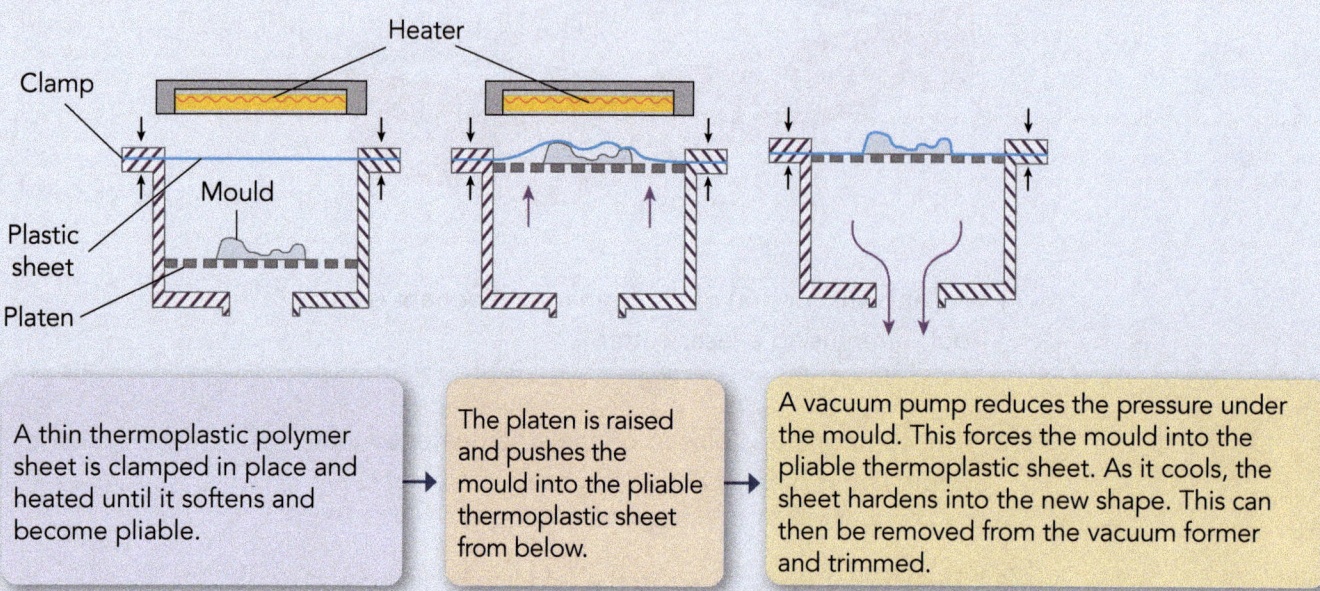

A thin thermoplastic polymer sheet is clamped in place and heated until it softens and become pliable.

→ The platen is raised and pushes the mould into the pliable thermoplastic sheet from below.

→ A vacuum pump reduces the pressure under the mould. This forces the mould into the pliable thermoplastic sheet. As it cools, the sheet hardens into the new shape. This can then be removed from the vacuum former and trimmed.

Mould characteristics

Vacuum forming moulds are made from a range of materials including MDF, wood and aluminium depending on their complexity and the number of times that they need to be used.

The shape of a mould needs to include a draft angle and avoid undercuts to ensure that formed components can be removed easily.

Vacuum formed shapes must be relatively simple:

- with no sharp corners that could cause tearing
- with no fine details that might not form properly (such as small lettering)
- with well-spaced features to prevent webbing
- with limited depth to prevent excessive thinning of the material.

Safety

- Do not touch the heating element.
- Do not touch heated material.
- Do not leave materials to heat up unsupervised.
- Allow formed material to cool fully before handling finished components.

Practise it!

Outline *two* limitations that need to be considered when designing vacuum formed products. **(2 marks)**

Remember it!

Vacuum forming:

- only works with thin sheets of thermoplastic materials
- is suitable for thin-walled components.

Forming processes: Moulding of GFRP composites see p. 79

What you need to know

- The tools, equipment, steps and safety measures used in moulding **composites**.

Glass fibre reinforced polymer composites (GFRPs) consist of strands of glass fibre held together in a polyester resin matrix.

Lay-up

Suitable for lightweight GFRP products with high strength to weight, such as canoes.

1. Release agent is applied to the surface of a single piece mould, usually made of wood or fibreglass.
2. A resin gel coat is applied, which will form the outer skin of the finished product.
3. Long strands of glass fibre often woven into matting are applied in layers and coated with polyester resin using a paint brush. A roller is used to compact each layer and expel any air bubbles.
4. Sufficient layers are applied to give the required strength and rigidity.
5. Once the resin has cured, the finished component is removed from the mould and trimmed.

Lightweight GFRP kayak manufactured using the lay-up technique.

Spray-up

Spray-up is quicker and easier than lay-up but results in greater wall thicknesses and more weight to achieve the same strength and rigidity.

Suitable for general purpose GFRP products, such as covers and panels.

1. Similar mould preparation and application of gel coat as in lay-up.
2. A mix of chopped fibres and polyester resin are applied to the mould with a spray gun to the required thickness.
3. A roller is used to compact the fibre/resin layer and expel any air bubbles.
4. Once the resin has cured, the finished component is removed from the mould and trimmed.

Close up showing random orientation of chopped strands typical of the spray-up technique.

Practise it!

Describe the difference between fibre alignment in GFRP composites made by lay-up and spray-up. **(2 marks)**

Remember it!

- GFRP stands for glass fibre reinforced polymer.
- GFRP composite is made up of glass fibres held in a polyester resin matrix.

Revision Guide

Forming processes: Moulding of CFRP composites see p. 79

What you need to know

- The tools, equipment, steps and safety measures used in moulding composites.

Carbon fibre reinforced polymer composites (CFRPs) consist of strands of glass or carbon fibre held together in a polyester or epoxy resin matrix. The image shows lightweight bicycle frames, wheels, seat posts and other components, all made from CFRP.

Vacuum bagging

Suitable for small, lightweight, thin walled CFRP products, such as racing bicycles, with exceptional strength to weight characteristics.

1. A wax release agent is applied to the surface of a single piece mould.
2. Woven carbon fibre sheets pre-impregnated with epoxy resin are laid into the mould.
3. This is then placed in a plastic bag and all the air is removed using a vacuum pump.
4. Inside the bag, the sheets are compressed together and forced into the mould.
5. This is then placed inside an autoclave where increased pressure and temperature is applied, causing the resin to cure.
6. Once the resin has cured, the finished component is left to cool, removed from the mould and trimmed.

Safety

Dust from trimming and finishing fibre materials and cured resins is harmful if inhaled.

The chemicals mixed to make resins are both toxic to humans and harmful to the environment.

Depending on the processes being carried out, PPE might include:

- eye protection
- respirator
- nitrile gloves
- disposable coverall with a hood
- disposable over shoes.

Revise it!
Create a short PowerPoint presentation to describe three methods used to manufacture fibre composite materials. Use appropriate illustrations sourced online.

Remember it!
- CFRP stands for carbon fibre reinforced polymer.
- CFRP composite is made up of carbon fibres held in an epoxy resin matrix.

Additive manufacturing: 3D printing see p. 80

What you need to know

- The tools, equipment, steps and safety measures used in 3D printing.

3D printing uses a computer model to manufacture a complex three-dimensional component from thermoplastic polymer.

Fused deposition modelling (FDM)

In FDM, specialist software is used to split a 3D computer model of the required component into thousands of thin slices. Each slice is then printed by a moving nozzle that deposits thin layers of thermoplastic polymer, one on top of another, until the component is complete.

The printer should have an enclosure to ensure that users cannot touch the heated nozzle, print bed or polymer and are protected from the heat and fumes from deposited materials.

PLA or ABS thermoplastic is supplied to the heated extruder unit from a spool of thin filament.

↓

The extruder melts the filament and forces it out of the nozzle at 190–285°C.

↓

Each slice of the model is recreated as a 2D layer of extruded polymer deposited from the nozzle.

↓

After each layer, the nozzle moves up to allow the next layer of polymer to be deposited.

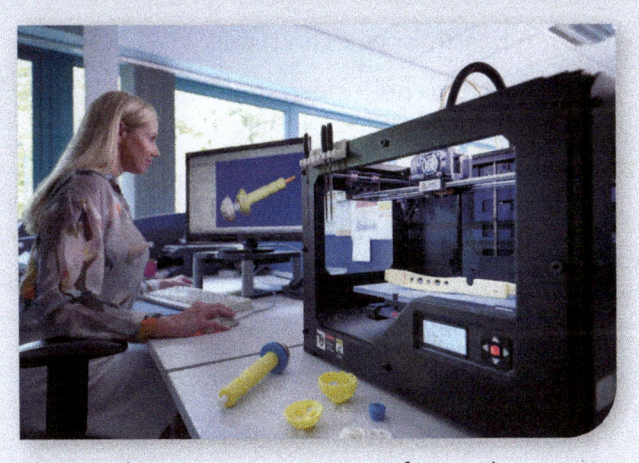

Simplified diagram of an FDM 3D printer.

Thermoplastic components manufactured using FDM.

Practise it!

Outline *one* important limitation of manufacturing components using FDM.
(1 mark)

Remember it!

- FDM stands for fused deposition modelling.
- FDM extrudes layers of thermoplastic to build up components slice by slice.

Revision Guide

Joining processes: Brazing see p. 81

What you need to know
- The tools, equipment, steps and safety measures used in brazing.

Brazing is a common method of permanently bonding steel (and other metal) components together.

Brazing

Brazing uses a brass **alloy** to bond or stick two components together. This differs from welding, which joins components by melting and fusing the parent metal together.

Thin-walled components like steel bicycle frames are brazed rather than welded as the lower temperatures involved prevent distortion.

The image shows brazing steel with an oxy-acetylene torch and a flux coated brass brazing rod.

Equipment

- Oxy-acetylene equipment (including torch, gas bottles, pressure regulators, etc.)
- Brazing hearth or welding bench
- Emery cloth (to help clean the surfaces being brazed)
- Brazing rod (often supplied complete with a layer of flux)
- Flux (applied to prevent oxidation which can prevent braze from wetting the surfaces being bonded) and to help the braze flow between the components.

Safety

- Care must be taken when carrying out any hot working process.
- Tongs must be used to move hot metal.
- Good ventilation is required to remove toxic fumes.
- Brazed components must be left to fully cool before handling.
- Brazing should be carried out away from flammable materials (including clothing).

PPE must include:

- gas welding/brazing goggles (Shade number 5)
- fireproof apron.
- gauntlets.

Practise it!
Explain *one* reason why brazing is used instead of welding on the thin-walled steel tubing used to manufacture bicycle frames.
(2 marks)

Remember it!
- Brazing uses a brass alloy to bond metal components together.
- Brazing bonds components together using surface adhesion. It does not fuse the parent metal like in welding.

Joining processes: MIG/MAG welding see p. 82

What you need to know

- The tools, equipment, steps and safety measures used in MIG/MAG welding.

Welding is a method of permanently joining similar metal components. MIG/MAG welding is a common form of gas-shielded electric arc welding.

MIG/MAG welding

MIG/MAG welding both use:

- an electric arc to provide the necessary heat to melt the component parent metal
- a spool of filler wire matching the component parent metal that is automatically fed into the weld pool (instead of using a welding rod)
- a shielding gas to prevent oxidation of the weld pool (instead of using a chemical flux).

MIG (metal inert gas) uses pure argon for shielding and is used for welding non-ferrous metals.

MAG (metal active gas) uses a mix of argon, and carbon dioxide for shielding and is used for welding steel.

Extensive PPE is necessary when carrying out MIG welding.

Safety

- Care must be taken when carrying out any hot working process.
- Good ventilation is required to remove toxic fumes.
- Welded components must be left to fully cool before handling.
- Welding should be carried out away from flammable materials (including clothing).
- Electric arc welding emits harmful UV light that can cause eye damage.

PPE must include:

- arc welding full face mask or helmet (shade number 10–14)
- fire retardant coverall
- fireproof welding apron
- welding gloves
- safety boots.

Equipment

- MIG/MAG welder (including earthing lead, welding torch, wire feed mechanism and shielding gas controls)
- Welding wire (matching component parent metal)
- Shield gas (gas bottle, pressure regulator and pipework)
- Anti-spatter spray (applied to surfaces around the weld to prevent weld spatter sticking)

Practise it!

What is the difference between MIG and MAG welding? **(1 mark)**

Remember it!

- Welding processes fuse together components made from similar materials.
- MIG/MAG welding uses an electric arc to generate heat that emits harmful UV light.

Revision Guide

Joining processes: Riveting   see p. 83

What you need to know
- The tools, equipment, steps and safety measures used in riveting.

Riveting is a method of permanently joining two or more overlapping metal sheets or plates. Riveting can be used to join dissimilar metals.

Hammered rivets
Hammered steel rivets are used on metal bridge structures, electricity pylons, boilers and water tanks although they have been replaced in many traditional applications by welded joints.

Hot riveting process
- Rivets are heated until they become red hot and malleable.
- A hot rivet is inserted into a hole through both components and held firmly in place.
- The other end is hammered (or peined) over, often using a pneumatic hammer.
- As the rivet cools it contracts and further tightens the riveted joint.

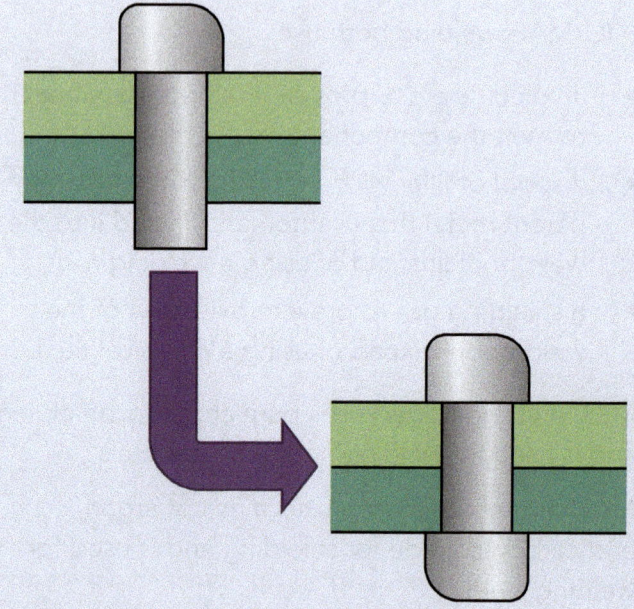

Rivets are inserted in a hole through two plates. Once hammered over (or peined) the rivet permanently joins two plates.

Pop rivets
Pop rivets can be inserted blind (with no access to the back side of the joint). They are used extensively in sheet metal work, for example, assembling enclosures, fixing hinges, attaching name plates.

Enlarged pop rivet — Rivet gun — Steel pin — Hollow rivet body — Pin breaks off — Completed rivet

Pop riveting process
- Insert rivet into a hole through both components.
- Use a rivet gun to pull the steel pin (mandrel) which collapses and expands the tubular rivet on the blind side of the joint.
- The steel pin breaks off when a pre-determined force is reached, leaving the rivet in place.

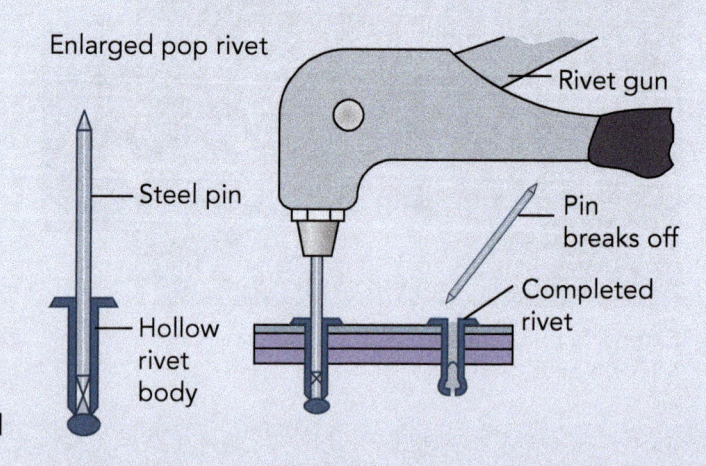

Practise it!
What is meant by the term 'blind riveting'? **(1 mark)**

Remember it!
Riveting is a permanent (or semi-permanent) method of fixing together sheet materials or metal plates.

Joining processes: Mechanical fastening see p. 83

What you need to know

- The tools, equipment, steps and safety measures used in mechanical fastening.

Mechanical fasteners allow components, including those made from different materials, to be joined together. They can be undone and removed to allow products to be disassembled.

Mechanical fasteners

Hexagon nut: nuts have an internal thread that screws onto compatible threaded components or bolts. **Tools:** spanner or socket wrench

Hexagon bolt: bolts have an external thread that screws into compatible threaded holes. They are often used in clearance holes with nuts and washers to join two components. **Tools:** spanner or socket wrench

Penny washer: flat washers are used with nuts and bolts to protect the surface of components and spread joining forces.

Pozi-drive self-tapping screw: self-tapping screws have a special hardened external thread that can cut a matching internal thread in thin sheet materials or thermoplastic components. **Tools:** screwdriver

Practise it!

Explain why non-permanent fasteners are used so commonly in mechanical assemblies and mechanisms. **(2 marks)**

Remember it!

Non-permanent mechanical fasteners include:
- nuts
- bolts
- washers
- self-tapping screws.

Revision Guide

Finishing processes: Painting and powder coating   see p. 84

What you need to know

- The tools, equipment, steps and safety measures used in painting and powder coating.

Finishing processes apply a coating to give the final colour to a product and to provide protection against corrosion.

Painting

Conventional wet paint contains coloured pigments and binders carried in a water or oil-based solvent. The solvent evaporates into the atmosphere as the paint dries and so must be used in a well-ventilated area.

Painting is widely used on a diverse range of materials (for example, metals, polymers, wood, concrete, and so on).

Application
Paint can be brushed on but a much better surface finish is achieved by spraying.

Paint spraying can achieve a high-quality surface finish.

Powder coating

Powder coating applies a highly durable and protective layer of polymer (polyester, epoxy) onto metal components without releasing solvents into the atmosphere.

Application
The metal component and dry powder are given opposite electrostatic charges.

This causes the fine power particles to be attracted to the metal and form an even coat.

The coated components move through an oven where the powder particles melt, fuse together and then cure to form a continuous coating.

Fine polymer powders are applied electrostatically before being cured in a baking oven.

Practise it!
State *one* environmental advantage of using powder coating instead of wet paint spraying. **(1 mark)**

Remember it!
Finishing processes are used to:
- apply colour
- provide protection against corrosion.

Strength, elasticity, ductility and hardness see p. 85

What you need to know

- The **mechanical properties** of materials (including their definitions).

The behaviour of a material under load (when forces are applied to it) depends largely on its mechanical properties.

Tensile strength

The maximum tensile (pulling) load a material can support without breaking.

Compressive strength

The maximum compressive (squeezing) load a material can support without breaking.

Yield strength

The maximum load a material can support and still recover its original shape when the load is removed.

Materials behave elastically until loaded above their yield strength at which point some permanent stretching will occur.

Ductility

The ability of a material to be permanently stretched without breaking.

High ductility materials like copper can be permanently stretched (drawn) into long wires using loads above their yield strength.

Low ductility materials (also known as brittle materials) like glass break almost immediately when loaded above their yield strength.

Elasticity

The ability of a material to recover its original shape after being stretched or compressed.

Springs depend on the elastic properties of steel to recover their shape. However, they can become permanently stretched (or compressed) or break if they are loaded past their yield strength.

A range of tension and compression springs.

Hardness

The ability of a material to resist indentation (dents) or abrasion (scratches and wear).

High hardness is often associated with high strength and low ductility (brittleness).

High speed steel (HSS) drill bits rely on high hardness and high strength to cut holes in softer materials like mild steel.

Practise it!

Which of the following best describes the behaviour of a material when loaded below its yield strength? (1 mark)
a the material breaks
b the material is permanently stretched
c the material behaves elastically
d the material stretches and then breaks

Remember it!

The key material properties to remember are:
Tensile strength   Compressive strength
Yield strength   Elasticity   Ductility   Hardness

Revision Guide

Malleability, machinability, cost and sustainability (see p. 86)

What you need to know
- Other properties of materials that influence manufacturing (including their definitions).

A range of other properties and characteristics can affect the choice of material used in a given application.

Malleability

> The ability of a material to be shaped by pressing or hammering without cracking or breaking.

Gold is highly malleable and can be beaten into gold leaf that is only 0.1 μm thick.

Material cost

> The cost of the material stock required to manufacture a component.

Engineers use the minimum quantity of material required to perform a task, to minimise material cost.

Manufacturing cost

> The cost of processing material stock into a finished component.

Engineers carefully select materials and processes to minimise manufacturing cost.

Machinability

> How easily a material can be machined (sawn, drilled, turned or milled).

Choosing materials with good machinability will make manufacturing easier and reduce manufacturing cost.

Using free cutting steels like EN1A can significantly reduce machining costs.

Sustainability

> The long term environmental and social impact of the extraction, processing and use of materials.

Raw material extraction and industrial processes that cause pollution and contribute to climate change must be minimised.

Recycled and renewable materials should be used whenever possible.

Revise it!
Make a series of flash cards and use them to help learn the definitions of the properties and characteristics of materials.

Remember it!
Engineers need to consider the long term environmental and social impact of the choices they make to ensure that they are sustainable.

Metals:
Ferrous metal alloys (see p. 87)

What you need to know

- The properties, typical forms of supply and common applications of ferrous metal alloys.

Pure metals are seldom used in engineering applications. Usually, metals and other elements like carbon are mixed at an atomic level to form metal alloys with enhanced material properties.

Ferrous metal alloys

Ferrous metals are alloys that contain iron mixed with small amounts of other alloying elements that change their material properties.

Ferrous alloy	Properties	Example applications
Low carbon (mild) steel – Carbon (0.15–0.30%)	• Moderate tensile strength (approx. 500 MPa) – higher than most non-ferrous alloys but lower than high carbon steel. • Ductile. • Cannot be strengthened or hardened using heat treatment. • Has poor corrosion resistance and will rust unless coated or painted; good machinability.	General purpose; widely used in a range of applications, for example, nails, staples, nuts, bolts, washers, car body panels, girders, steel beams.
High carbon (tool) steel – Carbon (0.8–1.4%)	• High tensile strength (approx. 900 MPa) higher than mild steel. • Can be strengthened and hardened using heat treatment. • Lower ductility than mild steel. • Has poor corrosion resistance and so will rust unless coated or painted. • Poor machinability.	Used in applications requiring high hardness, for example, saw blades, hammers, chisels, springs.
Cast iron – Carbon (2.0–3.5%)	• Low tensile strength (approx. 350 MPa) lower than mild steel. • Better compressive strength than mild steel. • Low ductility (cast iron is brittle). • Has poor corrosion resistance and so will rust easily unless coated or painted. • Poor machinability.	Used extensively for large cast components, for example, engineering vices, machine beds, engine blocks.
Stainless steel – Carbon (< 1.0%) – Chromium (>11.5%)	• Moderate tensile strength (approx. 600 MPa) higher than mild steel. • The majority of stainless steels cannot be hardened using heat treatment. • Lower ductility than mild steel. • High corrosion resistance. • Poor machinability. • Relatively expensive due to the high cost of alloying metals like chromium.	Used in applications requiring high corrosion resistance, for example, cutlery, medical equipment, kitchen sinks, chemical processing, food processing.

Practise it!

Explain why mild steel is not used for kitchen utensils such as knives and forks. **(2 marks)**

Remember it!

- The strength and hardness of ferrous metals is influenced mainly by their carbon content.
- Components made of high carbon steel (containing 0.8–1.4% carbon) can be heat treated to make them much harder.

Revision Guide

Metals: Aluminium alloys (see p. 88)

What you need to know
- The properties, typical forms of supply and common applications of non-ferrous metal alloys.

Non-ferrous metal alloys do not contain iron. Many common non-ferrous alloys used in engineering are based on aluminium.

Aluminium alloys

Aluminium alloys contain aluminium mixed with small amounts of other metals that change their material properties. They have much lower tensile strength than even mild steel but are around three times lighter.

Aluminium alloys	Properties	Example applications
Aluminium (>99.5% pure)	Very low tensile strength (approx. 75–105 MPa); high ductility; low hardness; moderate corrosion resistance; high electrical conductivity.	Electrical wire and cable.
Typical general purpose aluminium alloy – Copper (0.12%) – Manganese (1.2%)	Low tensile strength (approx. 90–160 MPa); high ductility; low hardness; moderate corrosion resistance; good machinability.	General purpose, sheet, cooking utensils, containers, pipes.
Typical structural aluminium alloy – Copper (0.28%) – Silicon (0.6%) – Magnesium (1%)	Low/moderate tensile strength (approx. 310 MPa) just over half that of mild steel; moderate/high ductility; low hardness; good corrosion resistance; good machinability.	General purpose, structural framework, furniture, ramps, stairs.

Forms of supply
Ferrous and non-ferrous metals are available in a wide range of standard bars, rods, sheets and profiles.

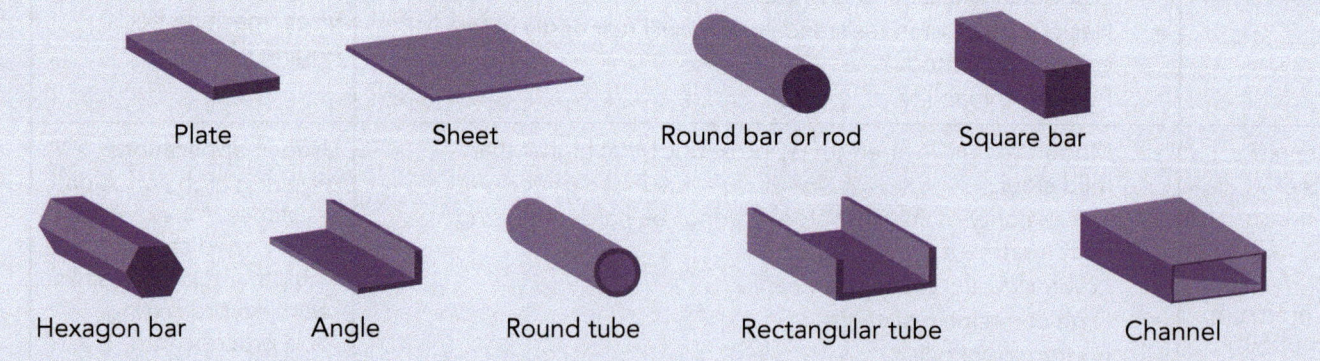

Plate   Sheet   Round bar or rod   Square bar

Hexagon bar   Angle   Round tube   Rectangular tube   Channel

Practise it!
Explain why high strength aluminium alloys are used to construct aircrafts even though aluminium has lower tensile strength than steel. **(2 marks)**

Remember it!
- Aluminium and its alloys are around three times lighter than steel.
- Use the bar, rod, sheet or profile that is closest to the final size and shape of the component you need to make.

Metals: Copper, brass and bronze see p. 88

What you need to know

- The properties, typical forms of supply and common applications of non-ferrous metal alloys.

Non-ferrous metal alloys do not contain iron. Many common non-ferrous alloys used in engineering are based on copper.

Copper alloys

Copper alloys contain copper, mixed with small amounts of other metals that change their material properties. Copper is a little better at conducting electricity than aluminium but is around three times heavier.

Copper alloys	Properties	Example applications
Pure copper (> 99.5% pure)	Low tensile strength (approx. 210 MPa); high ductility; low hardness; good corrosion resistance; very high electrical conductivity.	Electrical wire and cable.
Typical brass alloy: Cartridge brass – Zinc (30%)	Low/moderate tensile strength (approx. 270–480 MPa); high ductility; low/moderate hardness; good corrosion resistance; high electrical conductivity; very good machinability.	Pressed, deep drawn and spun components, for example, ammunition cartridges, fire extinguisher bodies.
Typical bronze alloy: Phosphor bronze – Tin (5%) – Phosphorous (<0.4%)	Moderate tensile strength (approx. 560–650 MPa) a little better than mild steel; moderate ductility; moderate hardness giving good wear resistance; very good corrosion resistance; high electrical conductivity; very good machinability.	Bearings, bushes, shafts, pump and valve components, springs, electrical switch gear.

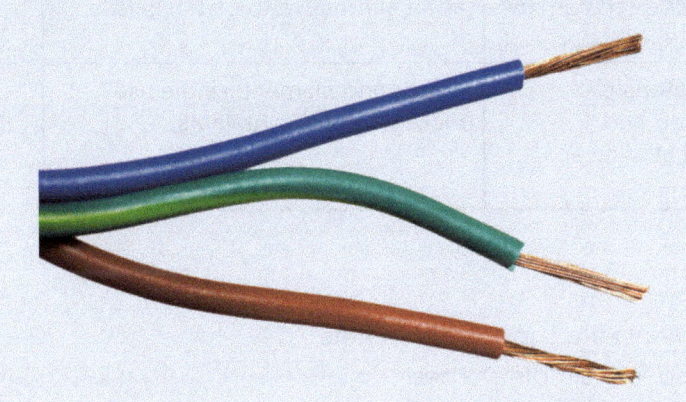

Copper is used extensively in electrical wiring because of its high elctrical conductivity.

Brass has very good machinability and is used in a wide range of mechanical components and fixings.

Revise it!

Make a spider diagram to summarise information on the properties and uses of copper and aluminium, and their alloys.

Remember it!

- **Copper** is an excellent conductor of electricity but weighs around three times more than aluminium.
- **Brass** is an alloy of copper and zinc.
- **Bronze** is an alloy of copper and tin.

Revision Guide

Polymers: Thermoplastic polymers (see p. 89)

What you need to know

- The properties, typical forms of supply and common applications of thermoplastic polymers.

Thermoplastic polymers are used extensively in a wide range of products because of their versatility, low cost and ease of manufacture.

Thermoplastic polymers

From toothbrushes to carrier bags, we all use thermoplastic products every day. Most are made from crude oil and so are not renewable but because thermoplastics can be heated and re-formed, they are straightforward to recycle. However, they are also a significant source of environmental pollution, especially in the world's oceans.

Polymer	Properties	Example applications
Acrylonitrile butadiene styrene (ABS).	Good strength; rigid.	Cases and enclosures for electrical products and electronic devices (such as computer keyboards, TV remote controls, printer components); waste pipes used in household plumbing; toys (such as Lego bricks).
High impact polystyrene (HIPS).	Good strength; moderate impact resistance; transparent unless mixed with coloured pigment or fillers.	Packaging; serving trays; storage boxes; bottle crates.
Polycarbonate (PC).	High strength; impact resistant; hard; transparent unless mixed with coloured pigment or fillers.	Safety glasses; exterior lighting; machine guards.
Polymethylmethacrylate (PMMA/Acrylic).	Good strength; low impact resistance; hard; transparent unless mixed with coloured pigment or fillers; excellent light transmission properties.	Baths; advertising signs; windows (as an alternative to glass); lenses.
Polylactic acid (PLA).	Sustainable (made from plant material); biodegradable (can be composted and will decompose.) can be shaped at a lower temperature.	3D printing filament; single use packaging and containers.

Forms of supply

Thermoplastic polymers for complex moulded components are supplied as pellets. Sheets of thermoplastic polymer can be cut and formed into simple shapes.

Practise it!

Which of the following is the most suitable thermoplastic polymer for use in the manufacture of safety glasses? **(1 mark)**

a PMMA
b PC
c ABS
d PLA

Remember it!

- Thermoplastics become soft when heated and can be easily moulded.
- Most thermoplastic polymers are made from crude oil and so have low sustainability.
- Waste thermoplastics that have not been collected for recycling are a significant source of environmental pollution.

Polymers: Thermosetting polymers see p. 90

What you need to know

- The properties, typical forms of supply and common applications of **thermosetting polymers**.

Thermosetting polymers are formed by permanent chemical reactions and cannot be reshaped once moulded.

Thermosetting polymers

Thermosetting polymers cannot be heated and reshaped and so are difficult to recycle. Most have relatively low impact resistance but maintain their high strength and rigidity even at elevated temperatures. They are resistant to heat, chemical attack and staining.

Polymer	Properties	Example applications
Urea formaldehyde (UF)	High stiffness, hardness and strength; good thermal and electrical insulator; resistant to heat, household chemicals and staining; opaque.	Electrical plugs, sockets and fittings; toilet seats; used as an adhesive in the manufacture of plywood and particle board.
Melamine formaldehyde	Good stiffness, hardness and strength; resistant to heat, household chemicals and staining; opaque.	Laminate coverings for kitchen worktops; impact resistant kitchenware and plates.
Epoxy resin	High strength; high stiffness; brittle; excellent resistance to temperature and chemicals.	Adhesives (to join dissimilar materials); used in fibre composite materials; industrial floor coverings.
Polyester resin	Good strength; good stiffness; brittle; good resistance to temperature and chemicals; lower cost than epoxy resin.	Used in fibre composite materials; car body filler.

Forms of supply

Thermoplastic polymers are supplied either as a powdered mix that requires heat and pressure to activate or as two-part liquids that must be mixed to start the chemical curing process.

Two-part liquid epoxy resin adhesive must be mixed in equal parts to start the curing process.

Practise it!

Which of the following thermosetting polymers is used as an adhesive in the manufacture of plywood? **(1 mark)**
- a epoxy resin
- b urea formaldehyde
- c polyester resin
- d melamine formaldehyde

Remember it!

- Thermosetting polymers are formed permanently by an irreversible chemical reaction.
- Thermosetting polymers do not soften when heated and cannot be remoulded.
- Thermosetting polymers are difficult to recycle.

Revision Guide

Engineering ceramics (see p. 91)

> **What you need to know**
> - The properties, typical forms of supply and common applications of engineering ceramics.

Industrial ceramics are incredibly hard and can be used as abrasive particles in grinding wheels or as solid tools made when fine carbide powder is fused together.

Engineering ceramics

Ceramic material	Properties	Example applications
Silicon carbide	- Exceptional hardness. - Moderate tensile strength. - Very high compressive strength. - Low density. - Extremely high melting point. - Chemically inert.	Abrasive papers; grinding wheels; cutting discs; ceramic brake disks; shot blasting media.
Tungsten carbide	- Exceptional hardness. - Moderate tensile strength. - Exceptional compressive strength. - High density. - Extremely high melting point. - Chemically inert.	Industrial cutting tools, for example, carbide lathe insert tooling, milling cutters and drill bits; abrasives.

Silicon carbide has long been used in carborundum cutting and grinding wheels.

Solid (tungsten) carbide tooling can be used to machine a wide range of materials with high material removal rates and long tool life.

> **Practise it!**
>
> Name a suitable material for use in lathe tooling inserts. **(1 mark)**

> **Remember it!**
> - Engineering ceramics are exceptionally hard with very high melting points.
> - They are widely used in cutting and grinding tools.

Composite materials see p. 92

What you need to know

- The properties, typical forms of supply and common applications of engineering composites.

Composites consist of particles or fibres (held together in a resin matrix) that provide enhanced mechanical properties when combined.

Types of fibre composite materials

Unlike metal alloys, each of the components in a composite remains separate in the microstructure of the material and retains its own mechanical properties. It is the combination of these individual properties in a single material that give composites their enhanced performance characteristics.

Composite	Composition	Properties	Example applications
Glass fibre reinforced polymer (GFRP).	Woven mats or chopped strands of silicate glass fibre in an epoxy or polyester resin matrix.	High strength; low density; high strength-to-weight ratio; difficult to recycle.	Kayaks and boat hulls; aircraft body panels; car bodywork repairs; bathtubs; water tubs; surfboards; roofing.
Carbon fibre reinforced polymer (CFRP).	Woven mats or long strands of carbon fibre in an epoxy resin matrix.	Extremely high strength to weight ratio and rigidity; more expensive than fiberglass.	Helmets, aircraft structures; lightweight sports cars; golf clubs; sports bicycle frames and wheels; tennis racquets.

The exceptional strength to weight ratio and rigidity of CFRP structures finds applications in cycling, motorsport and aerospace.

GFRP is widely used in offshore and marine applications including boat hulls and canoes.

Practise it!

What are the *two* key characteristics that make CFRP composite materials suitable for high performance applications in motorsport or aerospace?   **(2 marks)**

Remember it!

- Fibre composites consist of strands of glass or carbon fibre held in a resin matrix.
- GFRP stands for glass fibre reinforced polymer.
- CFRP stands for carbon fibre reinforced polymer.

Revision Guide

Smart materials see p. 93

What you need to know

- The properties, typical forms of supply and common applications of **smart materials**.

Smart materials can change their **physical properties** in response to a physical stimulus or change in their surroundings.

Types of smart materials

Smart materials can be metal alloys, polymers or composites.

Smart material	Properties	Example applications
Thermochromic pigment	Changes colour as its temperature changes; can be embedded in polymers and paints.	Thermometers; battery power indicator strips.
Photochromic pigment	Changes colour when its exposure to light changes; can be embedded in polymers and paints.	Sunglasses and lenses; glass in welder's masks.
Quantum tunnelling composite (QTC)	Composite of nickel particles held in a polymer matrix that changes from an insulator to a conductor when compressed.	Keypads; pressure sensors.
Shape memory alloy (SMA)	Nickel-titanium alloy that can be heat treated to set a particular shape; if that shape is bent or deformed, applying heat will cause it to regain its original shape.	Spectacle frames; stents; dental braces; robotic 'muscles'.

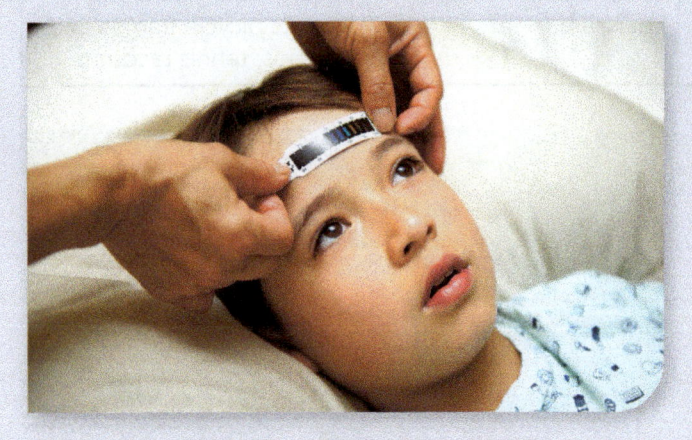

Thermochromic pigment is used in a low-cost polymer strip thermometer.

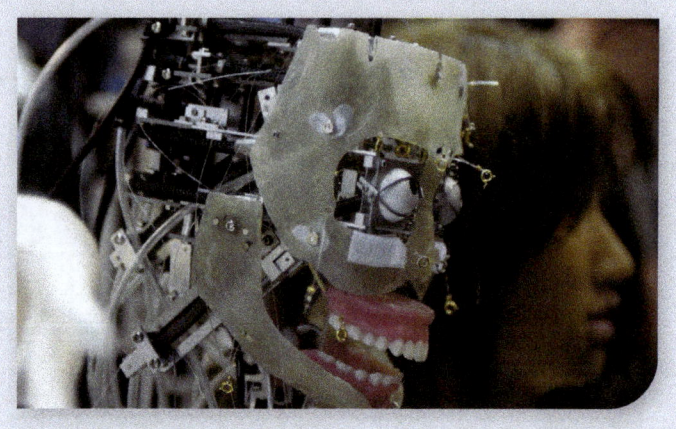

Shape memory alloy 'muscles' controlled by small electric currents can be used to control the movement of mechanisms and robots.

Practise it!

Name a suitable smart material that could be used in each of the following applications:

- A storage container that indicates the temperature of its contents **(1 mark)**
- Unbreakable spectacle frames **(1 mark)**
- To control thermal gain in buildings caused by strong sunlight shining through large windows. **(1 mark)**

Remember it!

Smart materials respond to a stimulus or change in their environment.

BS EN 8888 see p. 94

What you need to know

- How to interpret third angle orthographic engineering drawings to BS EN 8888.

BS EN 8888 represents an internationally agreed group of standards that are the dictionary for the visual language used in engineering drawings.

BS EN 8888

BS EN 8888 is an internationally agreed group of standards. Applying these standards means your drawings can be understood by engineers all over the world.

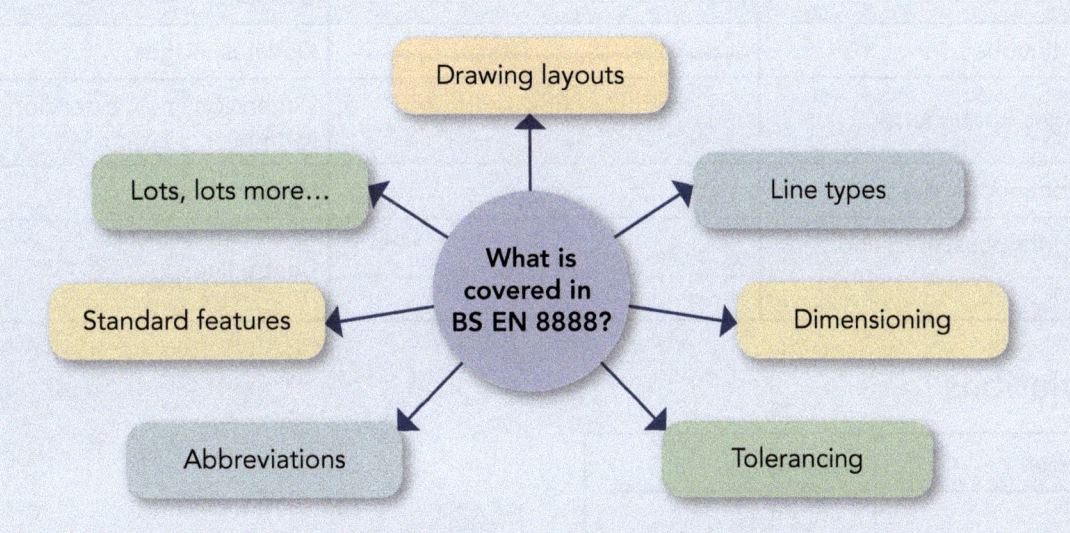

What is covered in BS EN 8888?
- Drawing layouts
- Line types
- Dimensioning
- Tolerancing
- Abbreviations
- Standard features
- Lots, lots more…

Third angle projection

The layout of the views or elevations of a component on an engineering drawing are usually arranged in a specific way called, **third angle orthographic** projection.

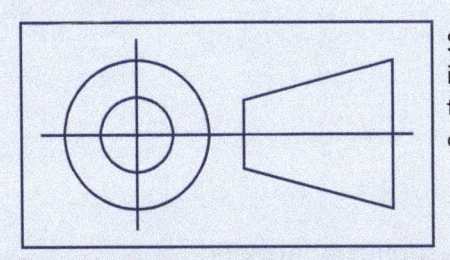

Standard symbol indicating a third angle drawing layout.

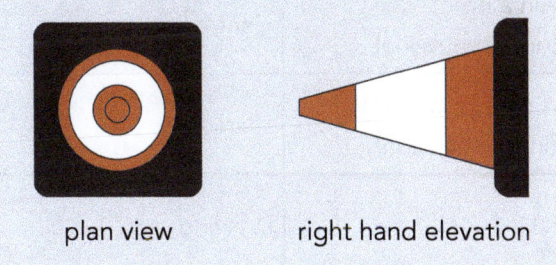

plan view   right hand elevation

This drawing of a traffic cone is laid out in third angle projection.

Revise it!

Sketch a series of household objects in third angle orthographic projection.

Remember it!

For your drawings to be understood you must use the standards and **conventions** laid out in BS EN 8888.

Line types and abbreviations see p. 94

What you need to know

- The meaning of line types and **abbreviations**.

Engineering drawings are packed with information. Even the thickness and type of line used has a specific meaning.

Line types

The line types used on drawings defined in the international standard ISO 128.

Line description	Example	Usage
Thick, continuous	——————	Outlines, edges
Thin, straight, continuous	——————	Dimension lines, extension lines and leaders
Thin, discontinuous, dash	- - - - - - - - - -	Hidden detail
Thin, discontinuous, long and short chain	—— - —— - ——	Centre lines

Abbreviations

Abbreviation	Meaning
AF or A/F	Across flats
CL (in a note) ₵ (on a centreline)	Centre line
DIA or D (in a note) Ø (in a dimension)	Diameter
DRG	Drawing
MATL	Material
SQ (in a note) ☐ (in a dimension)	Square

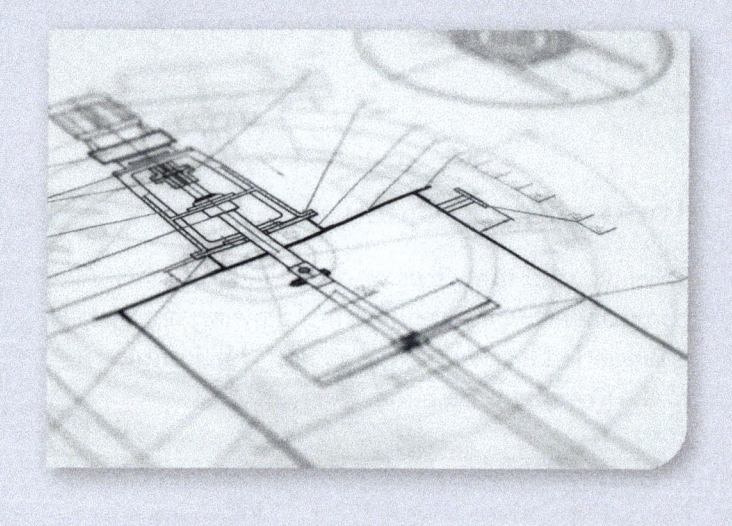

Although commonly seen on engineering drawings, abbreviated words should be avoided where possible as they are not immediately understandable in all countries across the globe.

Practise it!

What is indicated by the symbol Ø when seen on an engineering drawing? **(1 mark)**

Remember it!

Look closely at the line types used in an engineering drawing as they convey important information.

Dimensions, tolerances and surface finish see p. 95

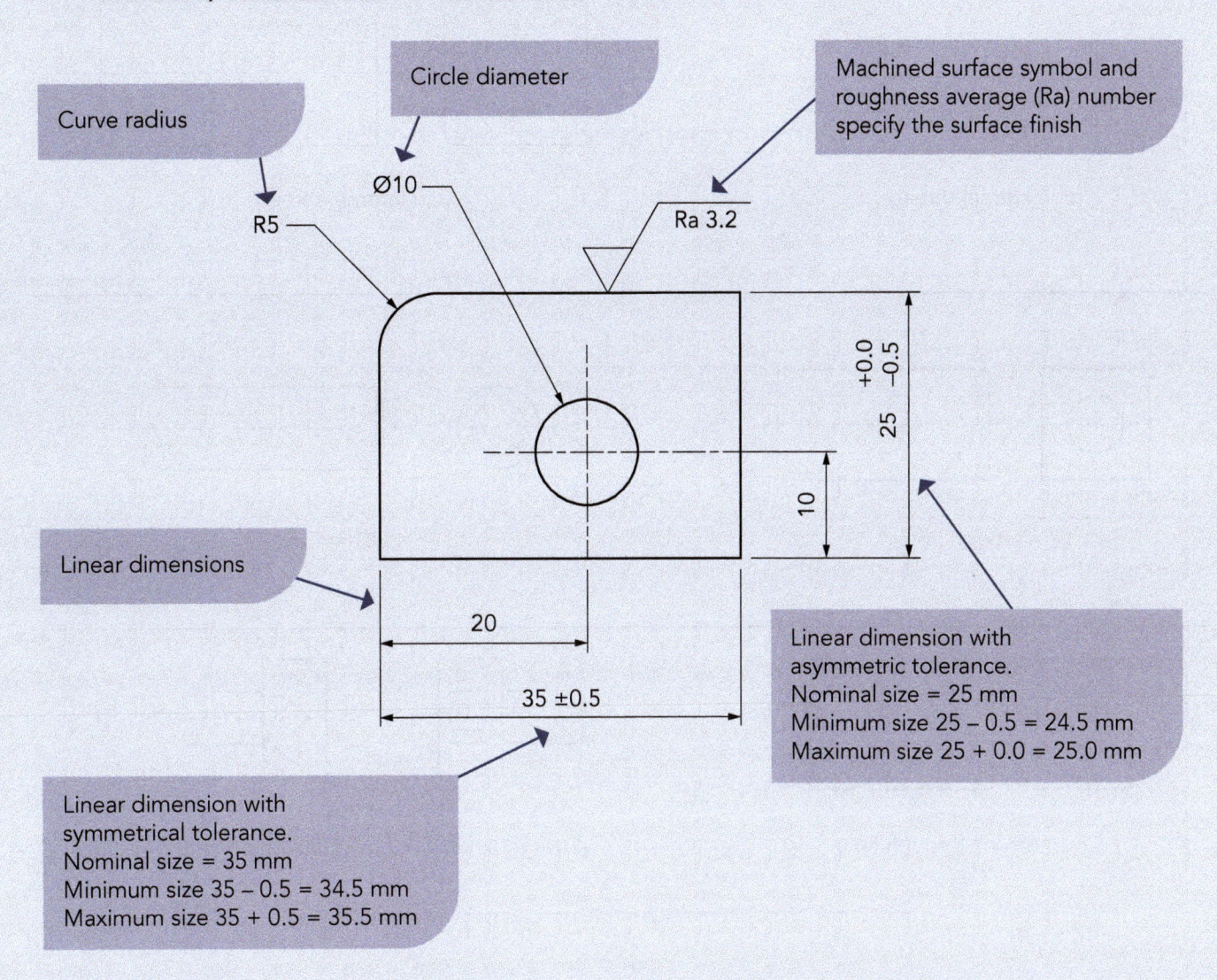

What you need to know

- The **standard conventions** for **dimensions** and **tolerance** calculations.

It is important to know how to read component dimensions and tolerance information on engineering drawings. Tolerances indicate the upper and lower limits that define the required accuracy for a component dimension.

Dimensions, tolerances and surface finish

Curve radius

Circle diameter

Machined surface symbol and roughness average (Ra) number specify the surface finish

Ø10

R5

Ra 3.2

Linear dimensions

20

35 ±0.5

10

25 +0.0 −0.5

Linear dimension with asymmetric tolerance.
Nominal size = 25 mm
Minimum size 25 − 0.5 = 24.5 mm
Maximum size 25 + 0.0 = 25.0 mm

Linear dimension with symmetrical tolerance.
Nominal size = 35 mm
Minimum size 35 − 0.5 = 34.5 mm
Maximum size 35 + 0.5 = 35.5 mm

Practise it!

Calculate the upper and lower tolerance limits for the following dimensions:

- 12.5 ± 0.25   **(1 mark)**
- 1100 +0 −5   **(1 mark)**

Remember it!

- Dimensions on engineering drawings in the UK are usually stated in mm.
- The accuracy required when manufacturing a component feature is defined by dimensional tolerances.

Revision Guide

Mechanical features see p. 96

What you need to know

- How to represent **mechanical features**.

It is important to be familiar with standard ways of representing common mechanical features.

Mechanical features

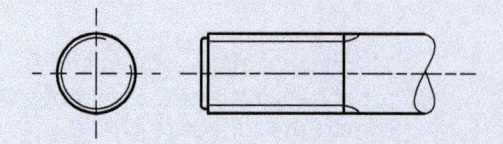

External thread

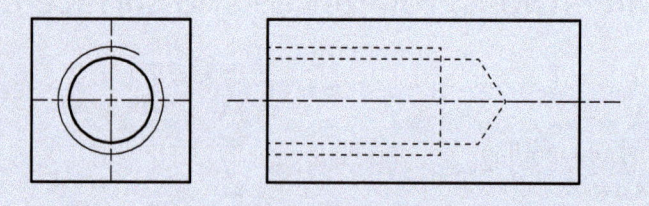

Internal thread

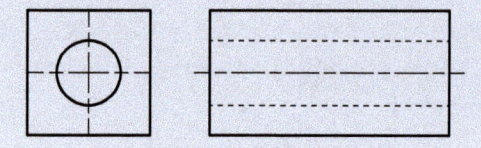

Through hole

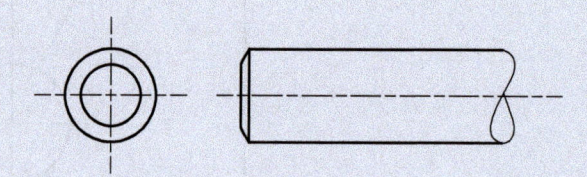

Chamfer

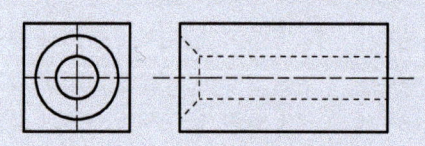

Countersunk through hole

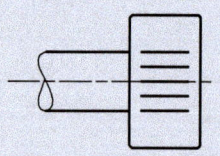

Straight knurl

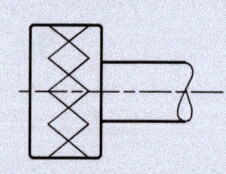

Diamond knurl

Practise it!

Describe the mechanical features shown in this drawing. **(3 marks)**

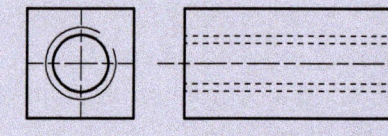

Remember it!

These mechanical features are good examples of how different line types are used in engineering drawings.

58 Revision Guide

Scales of manufacture (see pp. 97–99)

What you need to know

- How different **scales of manufacture** are used to produce a range of products
- How different levels of **automation** are used to manufacture a range of products.

The quantities in which products are manufactured has a significant impact on the tools, processes and level of automation that is used.

Scales of manufacture

	One-off	Batch	Mass
Production quantity	One	Low/Medium	High
Labour skill level	High	High/medium	Low
Labour cost	High	High/Medium	Low
Set up costs	Low	Medium	High
Manufacturing efficiency	Low	Medium	High
Product cost per unit	High	Medium	Low
Production rate	Low	Medium	High
Level of automation	Manual processes	Manual processes, **production aids** and **CAM**	CAM and fully automatic robotic control
Typical products	Prototypes, satellites, bespoke suits, made-to-measure kitchens	Baked goods, clothing, bicycle frames	Computers, mobile phones

Production aids

Production aids are used to speed up manufacturing and increase the repeatability of a manufacturing operation. On the downside, they can be time consuming and expensive to set up and are dedicated to a single product or specific operation.

Production aids	
Jigs and fixtures	Dedicated work holding devices: A fixture is permanently attached to a machine. A jig can be removed from a machine.
Moulds	Used for forming specific component shapes
Templates	Used for marking out and checking specific components

Practise it!

State two reasons why production aids are used in manufacturing processes. **(2 marks)**

Remember it!

Scales of manufacture include:

- **one-off**, such as satellites and bespoke suits
- batch, such as baked goods and clothing
- mass, such as mobile phones and computers.

Production aids speed up manufacturing and increase the repeatability of engineering operations.

Revision Guide

Computer aided manufacturing (CAM) see p. 100

What you need to know

- The advantages and limitations of using computer aided manufacturing (CAM).

Computer aided manufacturing uses computers to operate and control machine tools.

Computer aided manufacturing (CAM)

CAM uses 3D computer models to run machines that manufacture components

Advantages	Disadvantages
- One skilled setter/operator can supervise several CAM machines. - It has the ability to accurately machine complex shapes. - Human error is eliminated, leading to greater product consistency and fewer defects. - There can be an increased production rate. - It eliminates the need for operators to work in hazardous environments.	- CAM machinery is considerably more expensive to buy that manual equipment. - Fewer highly skilled manual machine operators are required, which can lead to job losses. - Because setter/operators need to be skilled, it leads to a limited staff pool. Additional training can take time and can have costs.

Revise it!

Create a short PowerPoint presentation to describe the advantages and disadvantages of CAM. Illustrate your slides with appropriate images sourced from the internet.

Remember it!

- CAM stands for computer aided manufacturing.
- CAM uses computers to automate machining processes.

Quality systems see p. 101

What you need to know

- The difference between **QA** and **QC**
- Why quality systems are used in engineering.

Quality systems are required to detect and prevent defects, reduce waste and lower costs.

Quality systems

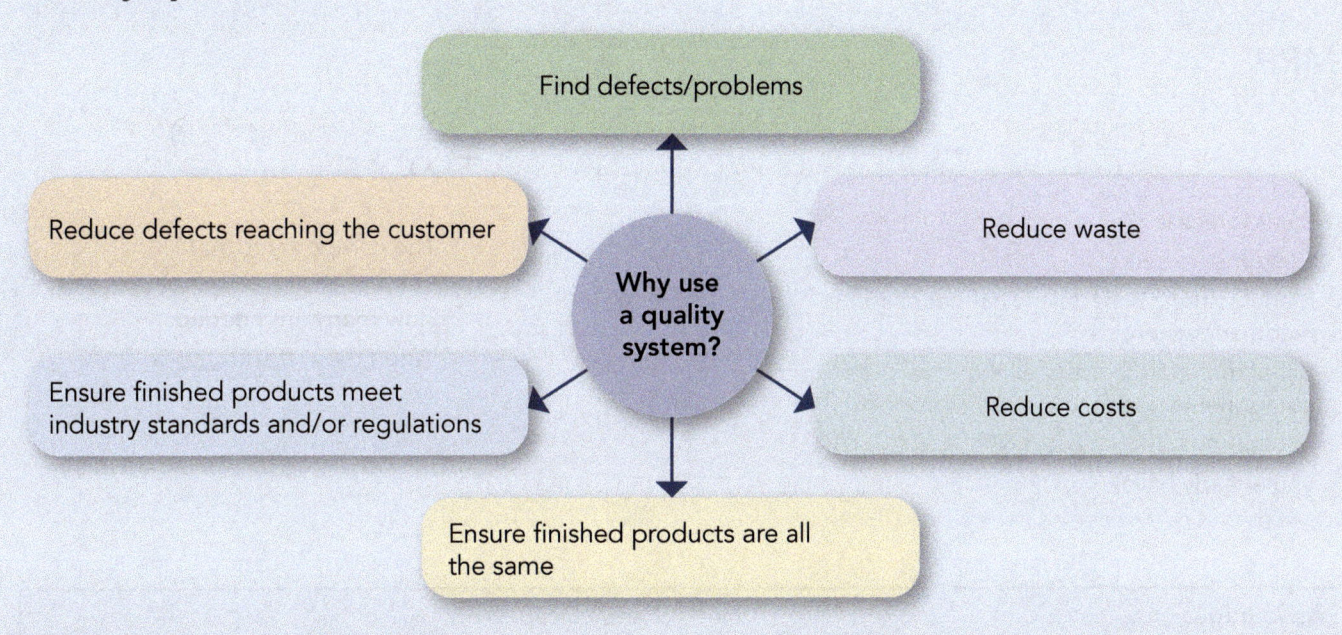

Why use a quality system?
- Find defects/problems
- Reduce waste
- Reduce costs
- Ensure finished products are all the same
- Ensure finished products meet industry standards and/or regulations
- Reduce defects reaching the customer

Quality control (QC) versus quality assurance (QA)

QC is a system of checks and measurements meant to **detect** defects/problems.

QA includes QC as well as a range of other activities meant to **prevent** defects/problems.

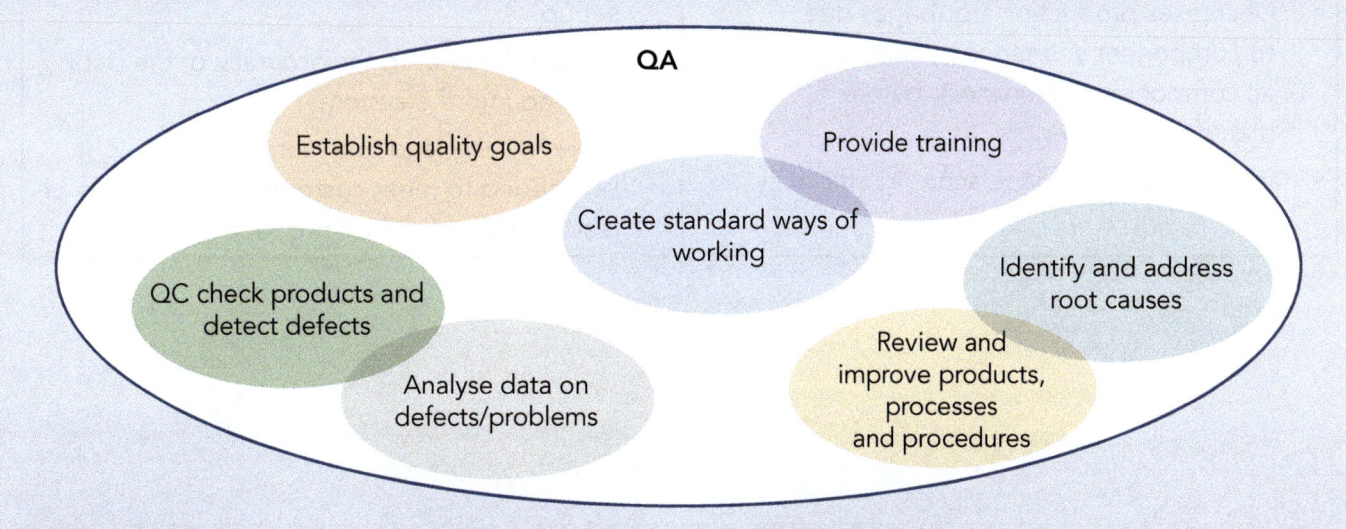

QA:
- Establish quality goals
- Provide training
- Create standard ways of working
- Identify and address root causes
- QC check products and detect defects
- Analyse data on defects/problems
- Review and improve products, processes and procedures

Practise it!

QC is a key part of every QA system.

List *two* other elements that might also be found in an effective QA system. **(2 marks)**

Remember it!

- QC is used to **detect** defects/problems.
- QA is used **prevent** defects/problems.

Revision Guide 61

Material requirements planning see p. 102

What you need to know

- The principles of **MRP**
- The advantages and disadvantages of MRP.

Material requirements planning (MRP) software is used to help manufacturers analyse the components they need, how many they should buy and when they need to arrive at the factory to be made into finished products.

MRP

INPUTS

Sales forecast
Customer orders
Manufacturing schedule (what needs to be made and when)
Bill of materials (a list of all the components needed to make a product)
Current **inventory** (any stock of materials you already have)

→ MRP system →

OUTPUTS

The components that need ordering
How many are needed
When they need to arrive

Advantages	Disadvantages
• Reduces the amount of component stock as it is purchased only when needed and is often used soon after it arrives. • Decreases production stoppages due to component shortages by ensuring all components are in stock before manufacturing begins. • Increases overall manufacturing efficiency.	• Reducing component stock limits flexibility in the manufacturing schedule. • The software is expensive and takes time to set up. • Results depend on the accuracy of the data entered into the system. • Stock of long lead time components might be needed to meet customer expectations of lead times for finished products.

Revise it!

Create a poster outlining the advantages of MRP aimed at small to medium sized businesses.

Remember it!

- MRP stands for material requirements planning.
- MRP helps to organise the components required to make finished products.

Just in time manufacturing see p. 103

What you need to know
- The principles of **JIT**
- The advantages and disadvantages of JIT.

JIT is a production system that lowers **production costs** by keeping stock of both components and finished products to an absolute minimum.

Just in time (JIT)

Traditionally, manufacturers held finished products in stock so that they could be delivered to customers immediately when an order was placed.

This meant large amounts of stock were manufactured and stored in large warehouses. This tied up money and incurred storage costs.

JIT is a production system designed to vastly reduce the need for holding stock. This stops money being tied up in components or unsold stock and means storage and warehouse costs can be minimised.

MRP systems are needed to enable JIT.

Customers expect short lead times and so the MRP timeframe must be compressed with component suppliers required to deliver components quickly and reliably.

JIT eliminates the need to hold stock which ties up cash and costs money to store.

Advantages	Disadvantages
• Reduces the amount of money tied up in components and finished products. • Reduces costs by reducing the amount of warehousing required.	• Requires cooperation from suppliers to reduce component lead times. • Vulnerable to any delay in component delivery. • Requires a flexible approach to production that allows frequent changeovers between products (JIT is often part of a **lean manufacturing** system). • Transition to JIT can be problematic.

Practise it!
State the *two* main advantages of implementing JIT. **(2 marks)**

Remember it!
- JIT stands for just in time.
- JIT is difficult to set up but allows businesses to save money by keeping stock levels very low.

Revision Guide

Seven wastes 1: Transportation, inventory, movement see p. 104

What you need to know

- The seven wastes of lean manufacturing: transport, inventory, movement.

Lean is a manufacturing philosophy that increases quality and reduces waste. Here, any activity that doesn't directly add value to the product being manufactured is considered waste and must be eliminated.

The seven wastes

In lean manufacturing there are seven categories of waste. It is important to know how reducing each waste improves the performance of manufacturing.

1 Transport	2 Inventory	3 Movement	4 Waiting
5 Over-production	6 Over-processing		7 Defects

Transport

Any unnecessary transport of components or finished products during manufacturing is a waste and adds cost.

Transport and handling also increases the chances of causing damage.

> **Action**: Optimise the layout of your factory so that parts flow directly from one process to the next.

Inventory

Excess stock of components or finished products ties up money that could otherwise be used to invest in the business.

The space needed to store excess inventory also adds unnecessary warehousing costs.

> **Action**: Use MRP systems and JIT to keep inventory to a minimum.

Movement

Any unnecessary movement by employees manufacturing a product is a waste and adds cost.

> **Action**: Optimise the layout of workstations, tools and equipment to minimise movement.

Practise it!

A worker must walk to the other side of a workshop to fetch their tools. Which type of waste would this be classified as? **(1 mark)**

Remember it!

Some forms of waste are not obvious and include transport, inventory and movement.

Revision Guide

Seven wastes 2: Waiting, over-processing, over-production, defects (see pp. 104–105)

What you need to know

- The seven wastes of lean manufacturing: waiting, defects, over-processing, over-production.

In lean manufacturing, any activity that doesn't directly add value to the product being manufactured is considered waste and must be eliminated.

Waiting

Whenever a product or component is not being worked on, it is waiting. This could be waiting for components to arrive or waiting to be moved between processes. Waiting increases the amount of money tied up in unfinished products and delays money coming into the business from sales.

Action: Optimise process design to allow continuous flow of work in progress.

Defects

Anything that affects the function or finish of a product that means it does not meet customer requirements and so cannot be sold (or is returned by a customer) is the most significant and obvious of the seven wastes.

Action: Use an effective QA system to manage and improve quality.

Over-processing

Producing finished items that are of a higher quality than is required by your customer is a waste.

Action: Understand the needs of your customer and the performance requirements of the product.

Over-production

Making more products than are required for immediate delivery adds unnecessary inventory.

Action: Use MRP systems and JIT to only manufacture what is required for immediate use or delivery.

Revise it!

Draw a spider diagram to summarise the seven wastes.

Remember it!

Some forms of waste are not obvious and include:
- waiting
- over-production
- over-processing
- defects.

Revision Guide

Globalisation (see pp. 106–108)

What you need to know

- About **globalisation** and its economic, social, ethical and environmental implications.

Good communication and transport links between countries have enabled the globalisation of the manufacturing industry where products designed in one country might be manufactured in another and then distributed to be sold worldwide.

	Implications of globalisation
Environmental	<ul><li>Additional transport requirements increase carbon footprint.</li><li>Environmental standard and limits on pollution are usually lower in low-cost countries.</li></ul>
Economic	<ul><li>Manufacturing in low-cost developing countries lowers product costs making companies more competitive.</li><li>Provides much needed income and growth in developing economies.</li><li>Imports must meet applicable international standards for quality and safety.</li><li>Imports can be affected by international trade restrictions, taxes and tariffs adding cost.</li><li>Long lead times can lead to the need to hold stock tying up money and incurring additional warehouse costs.</li></ul>
Ethical	<ul><li>Lower working conditions, lack of regulation, long working hours, no entitlement to breaks or paid leave and the use of child labour can all contribute to the exploitation of workers in low-cost countries.</li><li>Less strict health and safety regulations can lead to more industrial illness and injury in low-cost countries.</li><li>Low-cost imported goods can promote a non-sustainable disposable culture and trends like fast fashion where clothes are only worn once or twice before being discarded.</li></ul>
Social	<ul><li>Provides employment opportunities in low-cost countries but can lead to job losses in developed economies when production is moved.</li><li>Has the potential to increase the standard of living in developing countries.</li><li>Reduces inequalities between developing and developed countries.</li></ul>

Revise it!

Draw a poster containing researched images or photographs that illustrate the advantages and negative consequences of globalisation.

Remember it!

Globalisation pools global resources and manufacturing capabilities to lower production costs.

The types of manufacturing processes see p. 18

1 Explain what is meant by a 'wasting' process. **(1 mark)**

....

....

2 State *two* differences between forming and shaping processes. **(2 marks)**

1 ....

....

2 ....

....

3 Describe briefly how a product is made using an additive manufacturing process. **(2 marks)**

....

....

....

....

4 Give *three* reasons why finishing processes are used on products. **(3 marks)**

1 ....

....

2 ....

....

3 ....

....

Workbook

Wasting processes: Sawing, filing and shearing (see pp. 19–21)

1 State a type of saw typically used to cut the following. **(2 marks)**

(a) A straight cut through a metal bar.

Hacksaw

(b) A round shape in a sheet of polymer.

Coping Saw

2 (a) Describe how metal sheets are cut by shearing. **(4 marks)**

Metal is sheared between two offset blades, rather like scissors. It is held down by a clamp and the top blade is lowered onto the surface. As it touches the metal starts to push down.

(b) State *two* tools that can be used to cut sheet metal by shearing. **(2 marks)**

1 *Hack Saw*

2 *Tenon Saw*

3 Give *one* typical use of a file when manufacturing a product from metal. **(1 mark)**

68 Workbook

Wasting processes: Drilling, threading and routing see pp. 22, 23 and 25

1. Give *two* safety measures that must be used when using a bench-mounted drill to make a hole in a polymer sheet.

   For each give a different reason why it is needed.
   The first has been completed for you. **(4 marks)**

Safety measure	Why it is needed
Clamp down the material being drilled	To prevent the material spinning by holding it securely

2. Name the tool that is used to cut a thread by hand in the following applications. **(2 marks)**

   (a) A thread inside a drilled hole (internal).

   ....

   (b) A thread around a metal bar (external).

   ....

3. Give *two* typical uses of a router. **(2 marks)**

   1 ....

   ....

   2 ....

   ....

Workbook 69

Wasting processes: Laser cutting, turning and milling (see pp. 24–26)

1 State *two* safety measures that should be used when laser cutting. **(2 marks)**

1 ....
....

2 ....
....

2 (a) Describe how a round part is made by turning. **(2 marks)**

....
....
....
....

(b) State *three* safety measures that must be used when using a lathe. **(3 marks)**

1 ....
....

2 ....
....

3 ....
....

3 State *two* features on a product that are typically made using a milling process. **(2 marks)**

1 ....
....

2 ....
....

Shaping processes: Die casting (see pp. 27, 30)

1. The image below shows die casting equipment.

   Identify the main parts by matching the labels to the letters.

   One has been done for you. **(7 marks)**

| pressure chamber | cover die | plunger | ~~ejector die~~ | sprue | molten metal | cavity |

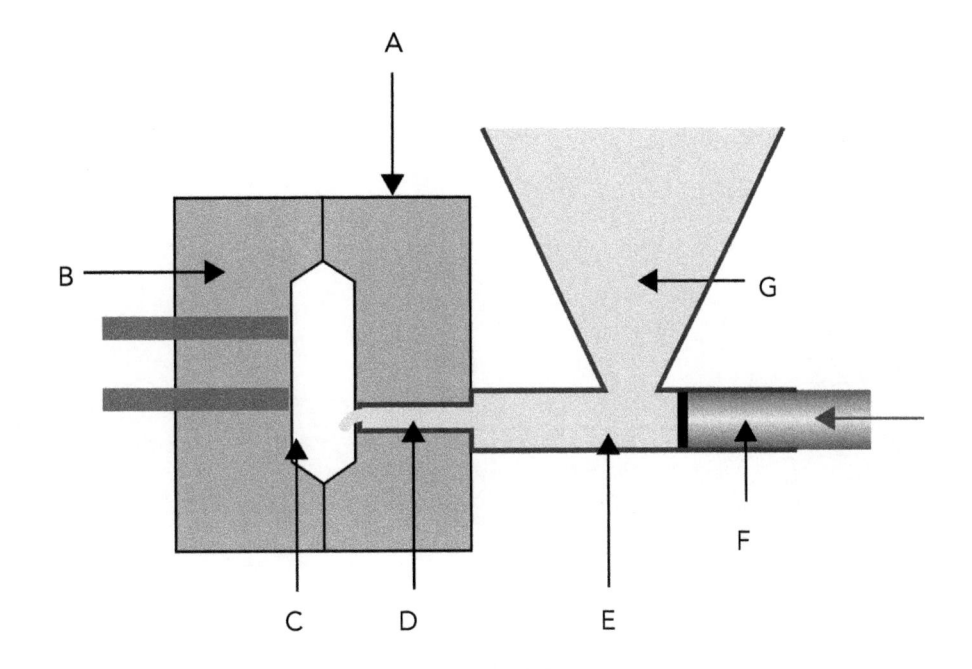

A		E	
B	*ejector die*	F	
C		G	
D			

2. State *three* ways in which the die casting process is different to sand casting. **(3 marks)**

   1 ....

   ....

   2 ....

   ....

   3 ....

   ....

Shaping processes: Sand casting see pp. 28–30

1 Using notes and sketches, describe how a mould is made for sand casting. **(9 marks)**

2 Explain the difference between a runner and a riser. **(2 marks)**

....

....

....

Shaping processes: Injection moulding   see p. 31

1 Label the main parts of this injection moulding machine. **(5 marks)**

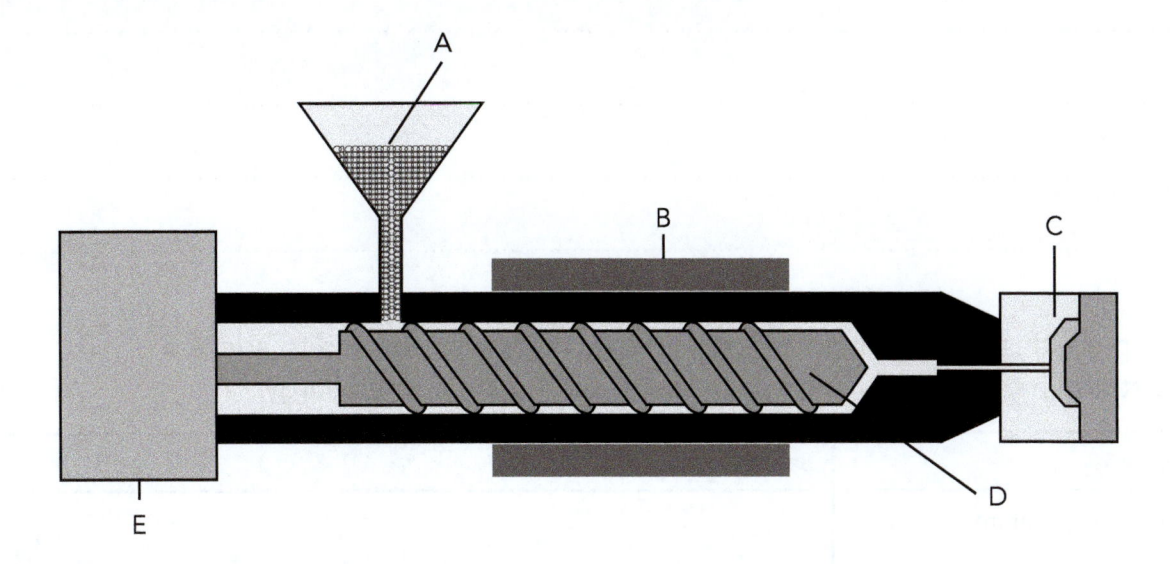

A	
B	
C	
D	
E	

2 Describe how a product is made by injection moulding. **(5 marks)**

....

....

....

....

....

....

Workbook

Shaping processes: Powder metallurgy (see p. 32)

1 Describe how a ceramic product is made using powder metallurgy. **(4 marks)**

....

....

....

....

2 Complete this table, giving a safety measure that must be used to address the stated hazard when making a product using powder metallurgy. **(2 marks)**

Hazard	Safety measure
High temperature	
Pressure	

3 State *two* ways in which the design of the mould for powder metallurgy limits the shape of the manufactured part. **(2 marks)**

1 ....

....

2 ....

....

Forming processes: Forging (see p. 33)

1 State *three* safety measures used when carrying out the forging process in industry. **(3 marks)**

   1 ....
   ....

   2 ....
   ....

   3 ....
   ....

2 Add labels to this diagram to identify the equipment used to carry out the industrial hot press forging of metal parts. **(4 marks)**

   A: _____
   B: _____
   C: _____
   D: _____

3 Describe how a metal part is made using the forging process. **(4 marks)**

   ....
   ....
   ....
   ....

Forming processes: Press forming   see p. 34

1. State the type and form of material manufactured using the press forming process. **(2 marks)**

   ....

   ....

2. Describe how the press forming process is carried out. **(3 marks)**

   ....

   ....

   ....

   ....

3. Complete this table, stating *three* hazards that can occur when press forming.

   For each, state a different safety measure that should be used. **(6 marks)**

Hazard	Safety measure

Workbook

Forming processes: Strip heating polymers (see p. 35)

1 State the type and form of material that is used with the strip heating process. **(2 marks)**

....

....

2 State *two* safety hazards that can occur during the strip heating process. **(2 marks)**

1 ....

....

2 ....

....

3 Describe how the strip heating process is carried out. **(4 marks)**

....

....

....

....

4 Explain *one* limitation of the strip heating process. **(2 marks)**

....

....

....

Forming processes: Vacuum forming see p. 36

1 Using notes and/or sketches, describe how the vacuum forming process is used to make a product. **(8 marks)**

2 Explain *three* characteristics of the moulds used for vacuum forming. **(6 marks)**

1 ....
....

2 ....
....

3 ....
....

Forming processes: Moulding of GFRP and CFRP composites see pp. 37–38

1 Complete this table, stating *two* safety measures that should be used when moulding a product from composite material. For each, give a reason why it is needed.
One has been done for you. **(4 marks)**

Safety measure	Reason
wear gloves	to prevent chemicals irritating skin

2 Using notes and/or sketches, describe how a product is made by moulding composite material. **(6 marks)**

Additive manufacturing: 3D printing (see p. 39)

1 Name *two* polymers that are commonly used to make 3D printed products. **(2 marks)**

   1 ....

   ....

   2 ....

   ....

2 Name *two* risks to health and safety that can occur when 3D printing. **(2 marks)**

   1 ....

   ....

   2 ....

   ....

3 Describe, in detail, how a product is made using 3D printing. **(6 marks)**

   ....

   ....

   ....

   ....

   ....

   ....

   ....

   ....

Joining processes: Brazing see p. 40

1. Complete this table, stating *three* health and safety hazards that can occur during brazing. For each, state a safety measure that should be used. **(6 marks)**

Hazard	Safety measure

2. Describe how the brazing process is used to join two pieces of metal. **(6 marks)**

....

....

....

....

....

....

3. Explain the purpose of the flux during brazing. **(2 marks)**

....

....

Joining processes: MIG/MAG welding   see p. 41

1 State what MIG stands for. **(1 mark)**

....

2 Label the main parts of the MIG/MAG welding equipment. **(6 marks)**

A		E	
B		F	
C			
D			

3 Explain three safety measures needed when carrying out MIG welding. **(6 marks)**

....

....

....

....

....

....

Joining processes: Riveting and mechanical fastening see pp. 42–43

1 Using notes and sketches, describe how two metal sheets can be joined using rivets. **(4 marks)**

```
┌─────────────────────────────────────────────────┐
│                                                 │
│                                                 │
│                                                 │
│                                                 │
│                                                 │
│                                                 │
└─────────────────────────────────────────────────┘
```

2 Give *two* advantages of using pop rivets to join two metal sheets, rather than standard rivets. **(2 marks)**

1 ....
....

2 ....
....

3 Name *two* tools that are typically used to put mechanical fastenings in place. **(2 marks)**

1 ....
....

2 ....
....

4 Give *two* advantages of using nuts and bolts to join metal parts together, rather than welding. **(2 marks)**

1 ....
....

2 ....
....

Workbook

Finishing processes: Painting and powder coating (see p. 44)

1 State *three* ways in which applying a finish can change the properties of a material. **(3 marks)**

1 ....
....

2 ....
....

3 ....
....

2 Explain *two* safety measures needed when spraying paint on a product. **(4 marks)**

1 ....
....
....

2 ....
....
....

3 List *two* materials often applied as a coating by powder coating. **(2 marks)**

1 ....

2 ....

4 Describe how a powder coat is applied to a metal product. **(4 marks)**

....
....
....
....
....

Strength, elasticity, ductility and hardness see p. 45

1 State what is meant by 'mechanical property'. (1 mark)

....

....

2 Which property means the ability of a material to resist scratches, indentation and wear? (1 mark)

....

3 Use sketches and notes to explain the difference between tensile strength and compressive strength. (4 marks)

4 State what is meant by 'yield strength'. (1 mark)

....

5 Explain the difference between an elastic material and a ductile material. (2 marks)

....

....

....

Workbook 85

Malleability, machinability, cost and sustainability (see p. 46)

1 State the meaning of the following properties.

(a) Sustainability (1 mark)

....

....

(b) Machinability (1 mark)

....

....

(c) Malleability (1 mark)

....

....

2 State *three* questions that an engineer might ask to determine the sustainability of a material. The first one has been done for you. (3 marks)

1 *Is the material renewable?*

....

2 ....

....

3 ....

....

3 Describe what is meant by 'manufacturing cost'. (4 marks)

....

....

....

....

....

86 Workbook

Metals: Ferrous metal alloys see p. 47

1 Explain what is meant by an 'alloy'. **(1 mark)**

   ....

2 For each of the following metals, state *one* typical application.

   (a) Metal: Cast iron **(1 mark)**

   Application: ....

   (b) Metal: Low carbon steel **(1 mark)**

   Application: ....

   (c) Metal: High carbon steel **(1 mark)**

   Application: ....

3 Explain why stainless steel is a suitable material to make knives and forks. **(4 marks)**

   ....

   ....

   ....

   ....

   ....

4 Describe how an increase in the amount of carbon affects the properties of carbon steel. **(4 marks)**

   ....

   ....

   ....

   ....

   ....

Workbook

Metals: Aluminium alloys, copper, brass and bronze see pp. 48–49

1 Explain what is meant by a 'non-ferrous' metal. **(1 mark)**

   ....

2 State *three* forms of supply in which metals are commonly available. **(3 marks)**

   1 ....

   2 ....

   3 ....

3 For each of the following metals, state one typical application.

   (a) Metal: Aluminium **(1 mark)**

   Application: ....

   (b) Metal: Copper **(1 mark)**

   Application: ....

   (c) Metal: Brass **(1 mark)**

   Application: ....

   (d) Metal: Bronze **(1 mark)**

   Application: ....

4 State *three* differences between the properties of steel and the properties of aluminium. **(3 marks)**

   1 ....

   2 ....

   3 ....

Polymers: Thermoplastic polymers (see p. 50)

1   State *two* forms of supply in which thermosetting polymers are typically available. **(2 marks)**

    1 ....

    2 ....

2   For each of the following thermoplastic polymers, state one typical application.

    (a) Polymer: Polycarbonate **(1 mark)**

    Application: ....

    (b) Polymer: Polymethylmethacrylate (PMMA/Acrylic) **(1 mark)**

    Application: ....

    (c) Polymer: Acrylonitrile-Butadiene-Styrene (ABS) **(1 mark)**

    Application: ....

    (d) Polymer: High Impact Polystyrene (HIPS) **(1 mark)**

    Application: ....

3   Explain why polylactic acid (PLA) is a suitable polymer to use for a single-use 3D printed product. **(4 marks)**

....

....

....

....

....

Polymers: Thermosetting polymers (see p. 51)

1 Explain the difference between thermosetting and thermoplastic polymers. **(2 marks)**

....

....

....

2 State *one* form of supply in which thermosetting polymers are typically available. **(1 mark)**

....

3 Describe the characteristic properties of thermosetting polymers. **(4 marks)**

....

....

....

....

....

4 Name *four* thermoplastic polymers. For each, state a typical application. **(8 marks)**

Thermosetting polymer	Typical application

Engineering ceramics see p. 52

1. State the typical properties of engineering ceramics. **(4 marks)**

   ....

   ....

   ....

   ....

   ....

   ....

2. For each of the following engineering ceramics, state *two* typical applications.

   (a) Silicon carbide **(2 mark)**

   Application 1: ....

   Application 2: ....

   (b) Tungsten carbide **(2 mark)**

   Application 1: ....

   Applicaton 2: ....

3. Explain *two* reasons why tungsten carbide is used to make surgical instruments. **(4 marks)**

   ....

   ....

   ....

   ....

   ....

   ....

Workbook

Composite materials (see p. 53)

1 Describe *two* differences between a composite material and an alloy. **(2 marks)**

....

....

....

....

2 State a typical application of glass reinforced polymer (GRP) and give a reason why it is preferred to other materials for that use.

Application: .... **(1 mark)**

Reason: ....

.... **(2 marks)**

3 Composites are finding increasing uses in high performance products.

Discuss what this could mean for the environment. **(6 marks)**

....

....

....

....

....

....

....

....

Smart materials (see p. 54)

1 Define what is meant by a 'smart material'. **(2 marks)**

....

....

....

....

2 For each of the following smart materials, state its smart property and *one* typical application. One has been done for you. **(8 marks)**

Smart material	Smart property	Typical application
Shape memory alloy (SMA)	*If deformed when cold, when heated it returns to its original shape*	*spectacle frames*
Thermochromic pigment		
Photochromic pigment		
Quantum Tunnelling Composite (QTC)		

Workbook 93

Line types and abbreviations (see p. 56)

1 What do the following line types mean on an orthographic drawing? **(5 marks)**

(a) ────────── ....

(b) ────────── ....

(c) ←────────→ ....

(d) ─ · ─ · ─ · ─ · ─ ....

(e) ─ ─ ─ ─ ─ ─ ─ ....

2 What do the following abbreviations mean on an engineering drawing? **(6 marks)**

(a) AF ....

(b) CL ....

(c) DIA ....

(d) DWG ....

(e) MTL ....

(f) SQ ....

Dimensions and tolerances (see p. 57)

1 Explain what is meant by 'tolerance' on an engineering drawing. **(1 mark)**

　..

　..

2 A dimension is stated on a drawing as 98 ± 1.5 mm. Ten components were measured and the results were:

| 98.7 | 100.5 | 96.5 | 97.3 | 99.4 | 99.6 | 98.5 | 96.9 | 97.8 | 96.3 |

Circle (O) any result that is outside tolerance. **(3 marks)**

3 On the drawing below, the dimensions are:

- length 30 mm
- height 20 mm
- distance from the bottom edge to the centre of the hole 10 mm
- distance from the left edge to the to the centre of the hole 22 mm

(a) Write in the dimensions in the correct locations. **(4 marks)**

(b) Add a dimension to show that the diameter of the hole is 12 mm. **(2 marks)**

Workbook　　95

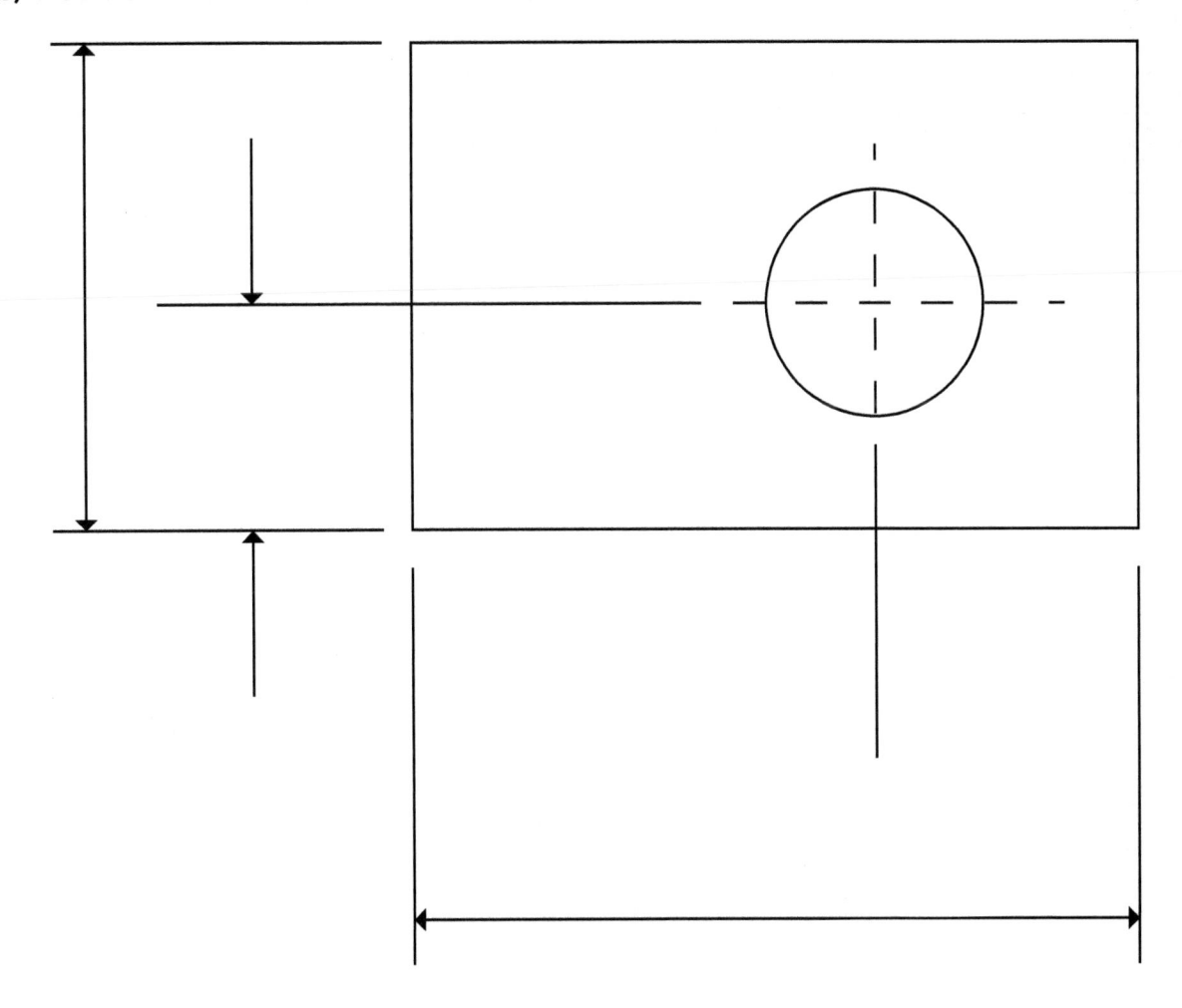

Mechanical features see p. 58

Identify the mechanical features shown in the following drawings. (7 marks)

1 ....

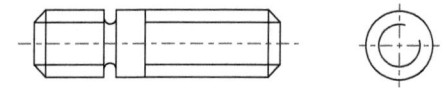

2 ....

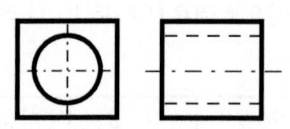

3 ....

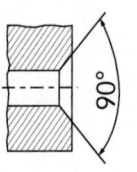

4 ....

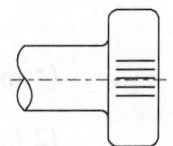

5 ....

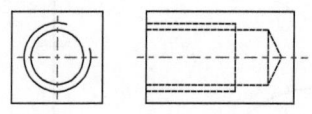

6 ....

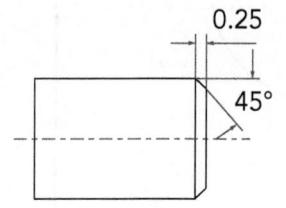

7 ....

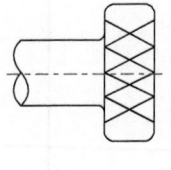

96 Workbook

Scales of manufacture see p. 59

1. State *two* typical characteristics of each of the following scales of manufacturing.

   (a) One-off manufacturing (2 marks)

   ....

   ....

   ....

   (b) Batch manufacturing (2 marks)

   ....

   ....

   ....

   (c) Mass production (2 marks)

   ....

   ....

   ....

2. Complete this list, giving *two* examples of different products made at the stated scale of manufacture. (6 marks)

   (a) Scale of manufacture: One-off

   Typical product 1: ....

   Typical product 2: ....

   (b) Scale of manufacture: Batch

   Typical product 1: ....

   Typical product 2: ....

   (c) Scale of manufacture: Mass

   Typical product 1: ....

   Typical product 2: ....

Workbook 97

Jigs, fixtures, templates and moulds see p. 59

1 Explain the difference between a jig and a fixture. (2 marks)

   ....

   ....

   ....

2 Give *two* typical uses of templates in a manufacturing company. (2 marks)

   1 ....

   2 ....

3 A company manufactures musical instruments in small batches.

   (a) Explain *two* potential advantages to the company of using production aids. (4 marks)

   1 ....

   ....

   ....

   2 ....

   ....

   ....

   (b) Explain *one* potential limitation to the use of production aids by the company. (2 marks)

   ....

   ....

   ....

Levels of automation (see p. 58)

1 Explain how the level of automation is affected by the scale of manufacture. **(2 marks)**

....

....

....

2 Other than machining processes, state *three* activities on a production line that may be automated. **(3 marks)**

1 ....

....

2 ....

....

3 ....

....

3 Complete this table, giving an example of products made using the stated level of automation and explaining why that level of automation is used. **(6 marks)**

Level of automation	Typical product
Manual	Product *Made-to-measure kitchen units.*
	Reason *This is a one-off bespoke, product with a high level of skill involved.*
CAM with operator	Product
	Reason
Fully automated robotic control	Product
	Reason

Workbook 99

Computer aided manufacturing (CAM) see p. 60

A company specialises in machining metal parts of complicated design.

Typical orders from customers range from a hundred parts up to a thousand parts, with each needing up to six different machining processes and paint spraying.

Currently, the company employs 45 highly skilled machinists and three paint sprayers.

Most machining processes are controlled manually.

To meet increasing demand, the company are considering introducing CAM equipment.

Discuss the advantages and disadvantages of using CAM to the company. **(12 marks)**

The advantages to the company would include...

100 Workbook

Quality systems (see p. 61)

1 Explain the difference between 'quality control' and 'quality assurance'. **(2 marks)**

....

....

2 Give *two* examples of quality assurance actions that a company may carry out. **(2 marks)**

   1 ....

   ....

   2 ....

   ....

3 A small company manufactures teddy bears for children.
Explain in detail why the company would want to implement a quality system. **(6 marks)**

....

....

....

....

....

....

....

Material requirements planning (see p. 62)

1 Describe what an MRP system does. **(4 marks)**

2 State *one* advantage to a company of using MRP. **(1 mark)**

3 State *four* limitations of using MRP. **(4 marks)**

1

2

3

4

4 Describe *two* characteristics of product demand in a company that might benefit from using an MRP system. **(2 marks)**

Just in time manufacturing (see p. 63)

1 Explain what is meant by 'inventory'. **(1 mark)**

....

....

2 What is meant by 'just in time' manufacturing? **(2 marks)**

....

....

3 A company manufactures parts for cars in large quantities on a production line using a make-to-stock approach.

It supplies the parts to the production lines of large automotive manufacturers (such as Ford, Peugeot and Toyota).

Discuss the potential advantages and disadvantages to the company of moving from a make-to-stock to a JIT manufacturing system. **(8 marks)**

....

....

....

....

....

....

....

....

....

....

....

....

....

....

Seven wastes: transportation, inventory, movement, waiting see pp. 64–65

1 Explain why a company may decide to use a lean manufacturing approach. **(3 marks)**

....

....

....

....

2 For each of the following, explain how it is a form of waste.

   (a) Transportation **(3 marks)**

....

....

....

....

   (b) Inventory **(3 marks)**

....

....

....

....

   (c) Movement **(2 marks)**

....

....

....

   (d) Waiting **(2 marks)**

....

....

....

Seven wastes:
Over-processing, over-production, defects see p. 65

1 For each of the following, explain how it is a form of waste.

   (a) Over-processing (3 marks)

   ....

   ....

   ....

   ....

   (b) Over-production (3 marks)

   ....

   ....

   ....

   ....

   (c) Defects (3 marks)

   ....

   ....

   ....

   ....

2 Give *one* example of over-processing when manufacturing a product. (1 mark)

   ....

3 Explain why a company might over-produce a product. (3 marks)

   ....

   ....

   ....

   ....

Globalisation: Part 1 (see p. 66)

1 Describe what is meant by 'globalisation'. **(3 marks)**

....

....

....

....

2 Explain, using an example, how globalisation changes requirements for transportation. **(4 marks)**

....

....

....

....

....

....

3 Explain *three* reasons why international standards are important for companies that use a globalised approach. **(6 marks)**

....

....

....

....

....

....

....

Globalisation: Part 2 see p. 66

A company manufactures garden furniture from wood. These are sold in the UK, France and Germany.

Currently, the company has small factories in each of these countries.

The company is proposing to move all manufacturing to a single large factory in China.

Explain how this proposal would affect the following.

1 Employment opportunities **(2 marks)**

....

....

....

2 The employment conditions of the workers **(4 marks)**

....

....

....

....

....

....

3 The cost of the product **(4 marks)**

....

....

....

....

....

....

Workbook

Globalisation: Part 3 (see p. 66)

A company manufactures sports shirts, as before, which are sold to fans. It currently has manufacturing sites in several European countries, each manufacturing shirts for local teams.

A consultant has suggested that the company should relocate their manufacturing to a single plant in India.

Discuss the economic, social, ethical and environmental implications of this proposal.

(12 marks)

Glossary

Key terms

Additive manufacture: Adds material layer by layer to build up the required shape of a component.

Abbreviations: Standard forms used to save time and space writing out the full word.

Alloy: A mixture of two or more metals, which has enhanced properties.

Assembly: A process of fitting components together to make a whole product.

Automation: The use of computers to control the operation of an activity.

Batch manufacture: Manufacturing products in specific amounts (a batch).

Composite materials: A material made from two or more different types of material, which can be identified separately within its microstructure.

Computer Aided Design (CAD): Allows 3D models to be produced on screen with different parts and modelled in different materials.

Computer aided manufacturing (CAM): The use of computers to control machining or assembly.

Conventions: Agreed rules or methods of presenting information so that everyone can understand it.

Dimensions: Numerical values used in engineering drawings to specify the sizes or positions of key features (measurements are usually in millimetres).

Ferrous metal: A metal or alloy which contains a high proportion of iron.

Finishing: A process that changes the surface of a material in a useful way, either protective or decorative.

Form (of material): The shape or nature of a material, for example, whether it is a sheet, bar, 3D shape, powder or liquid.

Forming: A process that changes the shape of a material without a change of state.

Globalisation: A process where companies source materials and manufacture products in different countries and transport them to their end markets.

Inch ("): Imperial measurement. 1 inch (") equals 25.5 millimetres (mm).

Inventory: The amount of materials, work-in-progress and finished products present in a company.

Just in time manufacture (JIT): Inventory arrives in a company only when it is required.

Joining: A process that is used to attach separate pieces of material together.

Labour cost: Cost of paying people to make the product.

Lean manufacturing: Manufacturing with maximum efficiency/minimum waste.

Manufacturing processes: Processes that are used to make products.

Material requirements planning (MRP): Helps to organise the components required to make finished products and a software-based approach used to manage inventory.

Mechanical features: Common features of a component's shape or form, such as holes, threads, chamfers, countersinks, knurls, displayed on drawings in a graphical method so that they are easy to identify.

Mechanical properties: Properties of a material in response to an applied force.

Millimetre (mm): Metric measurement. 25.5 millimetres (mm) equals 1 inch (").

Non-ferrous: Metal a metal or alloy which does not contain iron.

One-off production: Manufacturing products one at a time.

Orthographic (projection) drawings: Drawings that show an object from every angle to help manufacturers plan production. Uses several 2D projections (or views) to represent a 3D object.

Physical properties: Properties of a material that do not depend on an applied force.

Production aids: Devices used to simplify or speed up production or that help in making the product consistently.

Production cost: Overall cost of making a product.

Quality assurance (QA): Actions or procedures to prevent defects from arising during manufacturing.

Quality control (QC): A system of measurements or tests carried out to ensure a product is fit for purpose, for example, taking measurements to ensure that important dimensions are within the required.

Scale of manufacture: The quantity of product / parts to be made which determines the manufacturing process.

Shaping: A process that involves a change of state of the material.

Smart materials: A material that can undergo a reversible change in one or more properties in response to changes in its environment.

Standard conventions: Agreed rules that set the drawing standards used in engineering, i.e. BS EN 8888.

Thermoplastic polymers: A type of polymer that can be softened and re-shaped using heat engineering ceramics an oxide or nitride of a metal.

Thermosetting polymers: A type of polymer that cannot be reshaped when heated.

Third angle orthographic projection: A drawing showing three different views of a part in 2D (front, plan and side) on the same diagram.

Tolerance: The variation allowed between a specified dimension on an engineering drawing and the measured dimension on a finished component.

Waste: Any form of inefficiency or non-value added activity in a manufacturing company.

Wasting: A process that removes material.

Command words

Analyse: Separate or break down information into parts and identify their characteristics or elements. Explain the pros and cons of a topic or argument and make reasoned comments. Explain the impacts of actions using a logical chain of reasoning.

Annotate: Add information, for example, to a table, diagram or graph until it is final. Add all the needed or appropriate parts.

Calculate: Get a numerical answer showing how it has been worked out.

Choose: Select an answer from options given.

Circle: Select an answer from options given.

Compare and contrast: Give an account of the similarities and differences between two or more items or situations.

Complete: Add all the needed or appropriate parts. Add information, for example, to a table, diagram or graph until it is final.

Create: Produce a visual solution to a problem (for example: a mind map, flowchart or visualisation).

Describe: Give an account including all the relevant characteristics, qualities or events. Give a detailed account of.

Discuss: Present, analyse and evaluate relevant points (for example, for/against an argument).

Draw: Produce a picture or diagram.

Evaluate: Make a reasoned qualitative judgement considering different factors and using available knowledge/experience.

Explain: Give reasons for and/or causes of. Use words or phrases such as 'because', 'therefore' or 'this means' in answers.

Fill in: Add all the needed or appropriate parts. Add information, for example, to a table, diagram or graph until it is final.

Identify: Select an answer from options given. Recognise, name or provide factors or features.

Justify: Give good reasons for offering an opinion or reaching a conclusion.

Label: Add information, for example, to a table, diagram or graph until it is final. Add all the necessary or appropriate parts.

Outline: Give a short account, summary or description.

State: Give factors or features. Give short, factual answers.

Answers

The answer pages contain examples of answers that could be given to the questions from the Revision Guide and Workbook. There may be other acceptable answers.

Practise it! activities see pp. 18–66

Page 20
a 12" flat bastard file **(1)**

Page 21
d foot operated guillotine **(1)**

Page 23
taper → second cut → plug **(1)**

Page 24
Any *two* from:

- Laser cutting is far more repeatable and so capable of making batches of identical components (1)
- Laser cutting is much faster than cutting by hand (1)
- Laser cutting is more accurate than cutting by hand (1)
- A laser cutter can be operated by a low skilled worker and required no hand skills (1)
- Laser cutting will provide better material usage as the components can be nested closely together (1) **(2)**

Page 25
a vertical milling machine with face mill tooling **(1)**

Page 30
Sand casting **(1)**

Page 32
Sintering is the process of fusing closely packed metal particles together (1) at temperatures just below their melting point to make solid components (1). **(2)**

Page 34
Complex press tooling is expensive (1). This cost must be shared between the number of components the tool produces (1). To keep cost per component low, a large number of components must be produced (1). **(3)**

Page 36
Any *two* from:

- Sharp corners can cause tearing (1)
- Fine details might not form properly (1)
- Features too close to each other can cause webbing (1)
- Large depths can cause excessive thinning (1)
- Undercuts must (1) be avoided to allow removal from the mould
- Components must have a draft angle to allow removal from the mould (1) **(2)**

Page 37
Lay-up has a regular structure of long fibres or woven matting held in the resin matrix (1); spray-up has short, individual strands of chopped fibre in a random orientation (1). **(2)**

Page 39
Any *one* from:

- Components can only be manufactured from a limited range of thermoplastic materials designed for use with FDM (1)
- FDM is a slow process which limits production capacity. **(1)**

Page 40
Brazing is carried out at a lower temperature than welding (1) and so is less likely to cause distortion of the thin-walled tubing (1). **(2)**

Page 41
They use different shielding gases (1). (MIG uses pure Argon for welding non-ferrous metals. MAG uses Argon CO_2 O_2 mix for welding steel.) **(1)**

Page 42
Blind riveting only requires access to one side of the hole **(1)**.

Page 42
Non-permanent fasteners can be undone and removed easily (1). They are used in mechanical assemblies so they can be taken apart for servicing and repair (1). **(2)**

Page 44
Any *one* from:
- Powder coating does not release solvents into the environment (1)
- Powder coating generates less waste (1) **(1)**

Page 45
c the material behaves elastically **(1)**

Page 47
Kitchen utensils are exposed to damp, foodstuffs and household chemicals (1) which would cause mild steel to rust (1). **(2)**

Page 48
Aluminium is much lighter than steel (1). Weight is a critical factor when designing an aircraft (1). **(2)**

Page 50
b PC **(1)**

Page 51
b urea formaldehyde **(1)**

Page 52
Tungsten carbide **(1)**

Page 53
High strength to weight ratio (1)

High rigidity (1). **(2)**

Page 54
- thermochromic pigment **(1)**
- shape memory alloy **(1)**
- photochromic pigment **(1)**

Page 56
Diameter **(1)**

Page 57
- 12.25–12.75 **(1)**
- 1095–1100 **(1)**

Page 58
The drawing shows a length of square bar (1) with an internally threaded (1) through hole (1). **(3)**

Page 59
To speed up a process (1) and increase repeatability (1). **(2)**

Page 61
Any *two* from:
- Standard ways of working (1)
- Clear quality goals (1)
- Training (1)
- Data analysis (1)
- Root cause analysis (1)
- Review and improvement (1) **(2)**

Page 63
Reduces cash tied up in holding stock (1); reduces warehouse and storage costs (1). **(2)**

Page 64
Movement **(1)**

Answers: Practise it! activities

Workbook (see pp. 67–108)

Page 67

1. A process that involves cutting away or removing unwanted material to make a feature on a product. **(1)**

2. Any *two* from, for example:
   - Shaping processes involve a change of state/ forming processes do not involve a change of state. (1)
   - Shaping processes can make more complex shapes in a single step. (1)
   - Forming processes require force to be applied to the material to change the shape (1). **(2)**

3. The product is built up by depositing layers of material (1) progressively on top of each other (1). **(2)**

4. Any *three* from, for example:
   - To improve performance (1)
   - To increase corrosion resistance (1)
   - To increase hardness/abrasion resistance (1)
   - To allow a cheaper material to be used for the part by coating it with a more expensive material with the required properties (1). **(3)**

Page 68

1. (a) Hacksaw or mechanical hacksaw **(1)**
   (b) Coping saw **(1)**

2. (a) Two metal blades are placed parallel to each other (1) with a small offset between them (1). These apply force to the metal (1) which causes it to separate perpendicular to the blades/parallel to the blades (1). **(4)**
   (b) Tin snips (1), foot operated guillotine (1). **(2)**

3. Any *one* from, for example: to remove burrs (1), to round edges (1), to remove small amounts of excess material (1). **(1)**

Page 69

1. In addition to the answer given, any from the following:

Safety measure	Why it is needed
tie back long hair and loose clothing (1)	to stop entanglement in moving parts (1)
wear safety goggles (1)	to protect eyes from ejected swarf (1) **(4)**

2. (a) Tap (1)
   (b) Die (1) **(2)**

3. To cut thin material (1); to put a profile on an edge (1). **(2)**

Page 70

Any *three* from, for example:

1. Use of an enclosure around the process (1); extraction of fumes (1). **(2)**

2. (a) The workpiece is mounted in the chuck/ jaws of the lathe (1). It is rotated and the tool is moved against it (1). **(2)**
   (b) Use of guards (1); tie back loose clothing and long hair (1); wear safety goggles (1). **(3)**

3. Flat surfaces (1), grooves (1). **(2)**

Page 71

1. Place a flat sided half pattern (1) in the drag (1) and cover with green sand (1), applying pressure to ensure it is secure and sand is pushed into all features (1). Invert the drag (1) and place on the other half of the pattern (1) with sprue pins to allow for runners and risers (1). Cover the cope with green sand (1). Allow it to dry (1) Carefully split the drag and cope and remove the pattern and any sprues (1) before reassembling the mould ready for use. **(9)**

2. A runner is used for the metal to be poured into the mould (1); whereas a riser allows air to escape from the mould and excess metal to rise up from the casting (1). **(2)**

Page 72

1.
A	cover die **(1)**
B	ejector die
C	cavity **(1)**
D	sprue **(1)**
E	pressure chamber **(1)**
F	plunger **(1)**
G	molten metal **(1)**. **(7)**

2. Any *three* from: In die casting, the mould is typically made from metal, whereas in sand casting the mould is made from sand (1); the die casting mould is reusable, whereas the sand casting mould can only be used once (1).

   In die casting the metal is injected into the mould under high pressure, whereas in sand casting the metal is poured into the mould under the force of gravity (1).

   The equipment costs for die casting are typically much higher than for sand casting (1).

   Compared to sand casting, the cooling rate of the metal in die casting is typically faster (1), the surface finish is typically better (1) and there is typically less shrinkage of the cast item (1). **(3)**

Page 73

1. A: Hopper (1); B: Heater (1); C: Mould (1); D: Screw (1); E: Motor/Ram (1). **(5)**

2. Thermoplastic granules are placed in the hopper (1). As the screw turns it moves the granules along and they are melted by the heater (1). The ram provides pressure to inject the melted thermoplastic into the mould (1). Once cooled, the product is ejected from the mould (1) and excess material is cut away (1). **(5)**

Page 74

1. A ceramic powder metallurgy mix is placed in a mould (1). Pressure is applied (1) and the mould is heated (1). The surfaces of the powder particles melt and fuse together in the shape of the mould (1). **(4)**

2.
   - High temperature: Gauntlets/tongs/leather aprons (1)
   - Pressure: eye protection (1) **(2)**

3. For example, the product must have a slight slope on the sides/draft angle so it can be removed from the mould (1); it cannot include overlapping features (which would trap the part in the mould) (1). **(2)**

Page 75

1. Any *three* from: guards (1); safety glasses (1); tongs (1); gauntlets (1); leather/heat resistant apron (1); fireproof clothing (1); foundry boots (1); hearing protection (1). **(8)**

2. A: Ram (1); B: Punch (1); C: Die (1); D: Anvil (1). **(4)**

3. The metal is heated to red hot to make it malleable (1). It is then compressed into the shape of the cavity (1) by a ram applying hundreds of tons of pressure (1). Once cooled, excess material/flash from where the parts of the cavity meet is cut away (1). **(4)**

Page 76

1. Metal (1) sheets up to 6 mm (1). **(2)**

2. A sheet of metal is placed between two sides of a two-piece mould/former (1). A press then applies pressure (1) to force the metal sheet into the shape of the mould (1). **(3)**

3. For example:
   - Hazard: crushing fingers under the press (1); safety measure: machine guards / push button controls to ensure hands are not in the working area (1)
   - Hazard: cut fingers from sharp edges (1); safety measure: wear gloves (1)
   - Hazard: flying debris from broken parts (1); safety measure: wear safety glasses (1)
   - Hazard: cut toes/foot injuries from dropped sheets (1); safety measure: wear safety boots (1). **(6)**

Page 77

1. Thermoplastic polymer (1) sheets (1). **(2)**

2. Burns from hot material or the heating element (1); material catching fire/melting if left unsupervised (1). **(2)**

3. Any *four* from: A polymer sheet is made into a 2D net of the product (1). The line where the bend is to be made is placed directly over the heat source (1). When the material being bent reaches a suitable temperature, it becomes flexible along the heated line (1). It is then bent (1) over a former to achieve the angle needed (1). **(4)**

4. It can only make a simple bend in the product (1), as the heat is applied in a straight line (1). **(2)**

Page 78

1. Any *eight* from the following, as either text or annotated sketches: A mould is made in the shape of the product (1). This is placed on a platen inside the vacuum former (1). A sheet of thermoplastic polymer is clamped in place (1). The polymer is then heated until it is flexible (1). The vacuum is turned on and the air between the mould and polymer is sucked out (1). The pressure from the atmosphere pushes the mould into the polymer (1). As the polymer cools it hardens and stays in the shape of the mould (1). The mould is then removed and any excess material from the formed shape can be cut away from the product (1). **(8)**

2. Any *three* of the following statements, 1 mark for each characteristic and 1 mark for each reason: Should have a draft angle (1) to allow the mould to be removed from/slide out of the formed shape (1). Must have no overhanging features (1), otherwise these would lock the mould within the formed shape (1). Any edges must be rounded over (1) to reduce the risk of the plastic tearing (1). Often made from MDF or softwood (1) so the shape is not altered by the heating process (1). Features cannot be too deep (1) otherwise the plastic may become too thin when it is formed (1). Features cannot be too close together (1) otherwise webs may form between them (1). **(6)**

Page 79

1. Any *two* from, for example:
   - Safety measure: wear a face mask (1); reason: to stop breathing in of chemical fumes/fibres, which can harm lungs (1).
   - Safety measure: wear gloves (1); reason: to prevent chemicals irritating skin (1).
   - Safety measure: wear safety glasses (1); reason: to prevent small fibres that float in the air getting in eyes (1). **(4)**

2. Any *six* from the following, as either text or annotated sketches:
   - A mould is made in the shape of the product (1).
   - Layers of fibre are placed into a mould (1).
   - A mating part to the mould closes (1) and resin is injected (1). **OR** resin is applied by brush (1) and allowed to soak into the spaces between the fibres (1).
   - Heat and/or pressure may be applied (1) to cure the material (1).
   - Excess material from the edges is cut away (1). **(6)**

Page 80

1. PLA (1), ABS (1). **(2)**

2. Heat (from the melted plastic) (1); fumes (from the melted material) (1); electric shock (from the equipment if not used correctly) (1). **(2)**

3. A 3D CAD model is created (1). specialist software splits the model into lots of very small layers (1). The printer head moves in two dimensions to deposit each layer, starting at the base (1). It then moves up and deposits the next layer on top (1). The process is repeated until all the layers have been completed (1). **(6)**

Page 81

1. Hazards include: flames (1), hot metal (1), flux chemicals (1), combustible gases (1).

   Safety measures could include: use of fire bricks/forge (1), use of tongs to handle work piece (1), heat resistant gauntlets (1), use of gas pressure regulators (1), use of local exhaust ventilation (1).

Safety measure must be appropriate for the hazard for the mark to be awarded. **(6)**

2. The surfaces to be joined are thoroughly cleaned (1) and any oxides (rust) removed (1). Flux is applied (1) and the joint is heated with an oxyfuel flame (1). The brazing rod is added and melts (1), flowing into the gap between the parts being joined (1). When it cools, the braze solidifies, holding the parts together (1). **(6)**

3. It prevents oxidisation of the joint (1) and helps the braze to flow into the joint (1). **(2)**

Page 82

1. Metal inert gas **(1)**

2. A: spool of welding (1); B: gas regulator (1); C: gas cylinder (1); D: power source (1); E: return lead (1); F: welding torch (1). **(6)**

3. Any *three* from, for example:
   - Use of full face mask or helmet (high shade number) (1) to protect eyes from arc light (1)
   - Use of face shield/gauntlets (1) to protect face/hands from arc radiation or heat (1)
   - Use of local exhaust ventilation (1) to protect against fumes and gases (1)
   - Use of safety screens (1) to protect other people from arc light (1)
   - Use of tongs to move hot workpieces (1) protecting hands from heat (1). **(6)**

Page 83

1. A hole is drilled through both sheets (1). The rivet is heated and pushed through the hole (1) and the end hammered over (1). When the rivet cools, it contracts, helping to tighten the joint.

   This can be presented in text or as an annotated sketch. **(4)**

2. For example: Access is only needed from one side of the joint (1) and the process is quicker to carry out (1). **(2)**

3. Any *two* from: Spanner (1); socket wrench (1); screwdriver (1). **(2)**

4. The joints can be taken apart if needed (for example, to make a repair) (1) and no heat needs to be applied to the metal (1). **(2)**

Page 84

1. Improved aesthetics/appearance/colour/texture (1). Improved corrosion resistance (1). Increased resistance to scratches/hardness (1). **(3)**

2. For example: Carry out in a well-ventilated area / use local exhaust ventilation (1) to prevent volatile chemicals being breathed in (1). Wear a face mask (1) to prevent paint particles being breathed in (1). Wear safety glasses (1) to prevent paint particles entering eyes (1). Wear overalls (1) to prevent clothing being damaged (1). **(4)**

3. Polyester (1), epoxy (1). **(2)**

4. Up to *four* of: clean the surface of the metal (1).

   Particles are electrostatically charged (1) and sprayed onto the metal (1). The product is then heated to fuse the coating particles together (1). **(4)**

Page 85

1. Mechanical properties are how a material performs when a force is applied to it **(1)**.

2. Hardness **(1)**

3. Tensile strength is the ability of a material to resist breaking under a load that is pulling or attempting to stretch it (1), whereas compressive strength is the ability of a material to resist breaking under a load that is squeezing it (1). A sketch similar to the following, where the arrows indicate the forces (1 mark each for showing the tensile and compressive force):

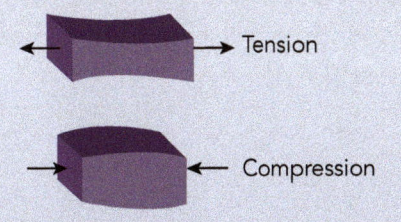

   → Tension

   ← Compression

   (4)

4   Yield strength is the load at which the material starts to permanently deform **(1)**.

5   An elastic material returns to its original shape when the forces applied to it are removed (1), whereas a ductile material is permanently stretched by a tensile force (1). **(2)**

Page 86

1   **(a)** Sustainability is the ability to use material from renewable or recycled resources **(1)**.

   (b) Machinability is the ease with which a material can be cut **(1)**.

   (c) Malleability is the ability of a material to be shaped by a compressive force without breaking **(1)**.

2   Any *three* from:
   - Is the material renewable? (1)
   - How much energy is needed to make the materials into a product? (1)
   - Can parts made with the material be reused? (1)
   - Can the material be recycled? (1). **(3)**

3   The manufacturing cost is the total cost of the equipment (1) plus the cost of the workers (1), which depends on the length of the process (1), divided between the total number of products made (1). **(4)**

Page 87

1   An alloy is a mixture of two or more pure metals. **(1)**

2   **(a)** For example, engineering vices (1) / anvils (1) / engine blocks (1) **(1)**

   (b) For example, car bodies (1) / screws (1) / nails (1) **(1)**

   (c) For example, saw blades (1) / hammers (1) / chisels (1) **(1)**

3   Stainless steel is hard (1) so it can cut through softer materials/food (1). It has good corrosion resistance (1) so food or washing will not mark it/cause it to rust (1). **(4)**

4   As the amount of carbon increases the steel becomes harder (1) and stronger (1), but less ductile (1). Steel with higher carbon content can also be heat treated to change its properties, whereas steel with low carbon content cannot (1). **(4)**

Page 88

1   Non-ferrous metals do not contain iron **(1)**.

2   Any *three* from: strip (1), bar (1), sheet (1), plate (1), angle (1), tube (1), channel (1). **(3)**

3   Any *one* from each:
   (a) Drinks cans (1) / aircraft parts (1) / pans (1) / window frames (1) **(1)**

   (b) Wire (1) / water pipes (1) **(1)**

   (c) Doorknobs (1) / pressure-valve bodies (1) / musical instruments (1) **(1)**

   (d) Statues (1) / cast products (1) **(1)**

4   Aluminium has better resistance to corrosion (1), lower density (1) and better strength to weight ratio (1) than steel. However, steel is typically less expensive (1). **(3)**

Page 89

1   Granules for melting and shaping (1); sheets for forming (1). **(2)**

2   Any *one* from each:
   (a) Safety glasses (1) / machine guards (1) / visors on crash helmets (1) / exterior lighting fixtures (1) **(1)**

   (b) Plastic windows (1) / lenses (1) / bathtubs (1) / advertising signs (1) **(1)**

   (c) Children's toys (1) / electrical housings (1) / keyboard keys (1) / plastic pipes (1) **(1)**

   (d) Food packaging / plastic cutlery / salad bowls / trays used in hospitals / electrical insulation **(1)**

3 It can be easily melted and deposited to form shapes (1) at lower temperatures than most other polymers (1). It is sustainable (1) as it is made from corn and sugarcane (1). It is also biodegradable (1) so will decompose much quicker than other polymers and can be industrially composted (1). **(4)**

Page 90

1 Thermosetting polymers cannot be reshaped once moulded (1) Thermoplastic can be heated, reformed and recycled (1). **(2)**

2 Chemicals that can be mixed together to make the polymer **(1)**

3 High stiffness (1), good or high strength (1), resistance to chemicals and staining (1), do not soften when heated (1). **(4)**

4

Thermosetting polymer	Typical application
urea formaldehyde **(1)**	One from: • Electrical sockets **(1)** • Casings for electrical appliances **(1)** • Coatings on fabrics to prevent wrinkling **(1)** • Wood glue **(1)** • Artificial snow (in films) **(1)**
melamine formaldehyde **(1)**	One from: • Laminate coverings for kitchen worktops **(1)** • Impact resistant kitchenware and plates **(1)** • Floor tiles **(1)**
epoxy resin **(1)**	One from: • Printed circuit boards (PCBs) **(1)** • Cast electrical insulators **(1)** • Adhesives (to join dissimilar materials) **(1)** • Ingredient in composite materials **(1)**
Thermosetting polymer	Typical application
polyester resin **(1)**	One from: • Suitcases **(1)** • Bonding or encapsulating other materials **(1)** • Ingredient in composite materials **(1)**. **(8)**

Page 91

1 Any *four* from:
- Corrosion resistant (1)
- Harder than most other materials (1)
- Low tensile strength (1)
- Good compressive strength (1)
- Very low ductility; not malleable (1)
- Brittle – can shatter on impact (1)
- Some glass ceramics can be transparent (1)
- Melt at very high temperatures (1)
- Glass ceramics can be recycled indefinitely (1). **(4)**

2 (a) Any *two* from: abrasive papers for sanding and polishing / wear plates / ball valve parts (1 mark for any appropriate example). **(2)**

(b) Any *two* from: lenses / glassware used in laboratories / drinks containers / windows (1 mark for any appropriate example). **(2)**

3 1 mark each for stating two reasons, with a second mark for the explanation:
- It is harder than most other materials (1), so it is able to cut them easily / retain a sharp edge when used (1).
- It is resistant to corrosion (1) so will not be damaged by bodily fluids or cleaning (1).
- It is resistant to heat (1) so will not be damaged by sterilising at a high temperature (1). **(4)**

Answers: Workbook

Page 92

1. A composite material is made by combining two or more different types of material whereas an alloy is made by mixing two or more metals (1). In a composite material the constituents can be seen separately in the microstructure, whereas in an alloy they are mixed at an atomic level (1). **(2)**

2. Applications could include: kayaks / boat hulls / aircraft body panels / car bodywork repairs / bathtubs / water tubs / surfboards, and the like. (1 mark for any suitable application.) **(1)**

   Reasons could include: higher strength / lower density / higher strength to weight ratio than metals (1) so offers reduced weight of the manufactured item, which could allow better performance (1). **(2)**

3. Any *six* from, for example: Composites cannot be recycled (1) as the two constituents cannot be easily separated (1). This means that most end up in landfill at the end of their life (1), which uses up valuable resources (1) and could cause damage to local ecosystems / pollution (1). As they typically contain polymers, they do not biodegrade easily (1), so last for a long time (1). This means that the increased use of composites may not be good for the environment (1). However, the better properties of composites may mean that fewer of them are needed and they last longer than the materials they replace (1), which could reduce the environmental impact overall (1). **(6)**

Page 93

1. A material where one or more properties change when there is a change in its environment (1); this change is reversible when the environment changes again (1). **(2)**

2. Shape memory alloy – property: if deformed when cold, when heated it returns to its original shape (1) – applications include: spectacle frames (1)

   Thermochromic pigment – property: changes colour with temperature (1) – applications include plastic thermometers / food packaging that changes colour when the food is the right temperature / battery power indicator strips / colour change paint for nursery walls (1 mark for any typical application).

   Photochromic pigment – property: changes colour when the light level changes (1) – applications include sunglasses and lenses / security marking (inks that show under ultraviolet light) / glass used in welder's masks / cosmetics (colour changing nail varnish) / clothing / car body paint (1 mark for any typical application).

   Quantum tunnelling composite (QTC) – property: changes from an insulator to a conductor when squeezed (1) – applications include keypads / pressure pads (for example, sensors for alarm systems) / training dummies for martial arts and fencing/sword fighting (1 mark for any typical application). **(8)**

Page 94

1. (a) Outline (1)

   (b) Extension or leader line (1)

   (c) Dimension line (1)

   (d) Centre line (1)

   (e) Hidden detail (1) **(5)**

2. (a) Across flats (1)

   (b) Centre line (1)

   (c) Diameter (1)

   (d) Drawing (1)

   (e) Material (1)

   (f) Square (1) **(5)**

Page 95

1. The maximum acceptable variation from the ideal dimension **(1)**

2. Values circled should be: **100.5**, **99.6** and **96.3** (1 mark for each correctly circled value – deduct 1 mark for circling any measurement that is in tolerance). **(3)**

3 (a) 1 mark for each correctly placed dimension (for example, 30 is above the line in a central position). **(4)**

(b) 1 mark for adding an appropriate dimensioning line (or lines) for the diameter and 1 mark for positioning the value correctly. **(2)**

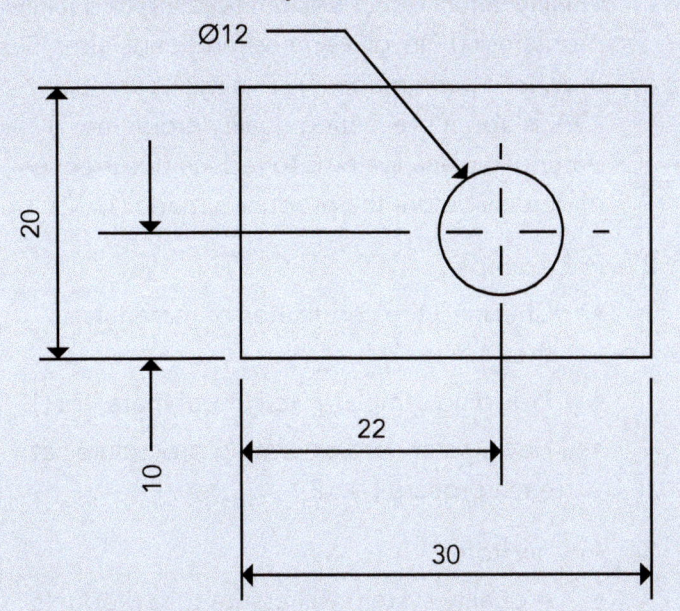

Page 96

1. External thread (1)
2. Through holes (1)
3. Countersink (1)
4. Straight knurls (1)
5. Internal thread into a blind hole (1)
6. Chamfer (1)
7. Diamond knurls. (1) **(7)**

Page 97

1. Any *two* from each, for example:
   (a) Manual processes / low level of automation (1); high level of operator skill (1); higher labour content in production than other scales of manufacture (1); machines must be flexible/can be switched between different tasks or products (1). **(2)**

   (b) May have a mixture of manual and automated processes (1); products are made in set quantities before switching to another product (1); some customisation of products possible (in batches) (1); commonly involves use of jigs, fixtures and templates (1). **(2)**

   (c) High level of automation (1); high capital costs (1); use of lower skilled workers (1); products are standardised (1); typically labour time per product lower than other scales (1); often organised as production lines (1) with equipment dedicated to carrying out single tasks (1). **(2)**

2. Any *two* from each, for example:
   (a) one-off: tailored suit (1) / satellite (1) / statues (1) / replacements for broken parts (1);

   (b) batch: furniture sold in high street stores (1) / skateboards (1) / books (1);

   (c) mass: mobile phones (1) / cars (1) / chocolate bars (1) / nuts and bolts (1). **(6)**

Page 98

1. A fixture is permanently attached to the base/bed of the machine (1), whereas a jig can be easily removed (1). **(2)**

2. Marking out (1), checking that the size of manufactured parts is correct (1). **(2)**

3. (a) • Reduced time to mark out (1) reduces labour costs per product (1);
   • improved consistency / repeatability of products in a batch (1) resulting in less waste / better quality (1). **(4)**

   (b) The cost involved in making the production aid (1) could exceed the time saved by using it (1). **(2)**

Page 99

1. Use of automation normally increases as the number of parts to be made increases (1), as the cost of the equipment can be divided between many products (1). **(2)**

2. Loading/unloading machines (1); moving products between processes (1); measurement activities (1). **(3)**

Answers: Workbook

3   1 mark for each product and 1 mark for each reason, for example:

Manual:

Product: tailored suit (1) / replacements for broken parts (1).

Reason: the time and cost to set up CAM equipment would be greater than any saving from using CAM (1).

CAM with operator:

Product: furniture sold in high street stores (1) / skateboards (1) / books (1).

Reason: to ensure that products are similar (1) / to maintain quality standards, whilst still having flexibility to switch between products (1).

Fully automated:

Product: mobile phones (1) / cars (1) / nuts and bolts (1).

Reason: the cost of the equipment can be divided between many products (1). **(6)**

Page 100

Any *twelve* from, for example: Potential advantages

- Faster rate of production / greater output (1)
- Improved consistency of products (1)
- Less human error: reduction in defects (1)
- Able to accurately manufacture complex parts (1)
- May offer less hazards to workers if used in environments that are hazardous to humans (1) such as spray painting (1)
- Employment opportunities for programming (1) and maintaining the equipment (1)
- Potential to reduce labour costs (1) by using some lower-skilled staff to 'mind' CAM processes (1)

Disadvantages

- May cause resentment from current highly-skilled staff (1), who would need retraining to use the CAM processes (1)
- High equipment cost / capital outlay (1)
- Equipment still needs to be flexible enough to switch between batches (1)
- Relies on consistency (1) – must receive similar products every time but there may be big variations between batches (1)
- Can be difficult to change the function of the equipment / need for reprogramming between batches (1). **(12)**

Page 101

1   Any *one* from each system, for example: Quality control (QC) is about reacting to quality problems (1) / involves measuring parts after they have been made (1). Quality Assurance (QA) is about preventing quality problems (1) / putting in place systems to reduce occurrence of defects before the product is made (1). **(2)**

2   For example:
- Checking the certificates of materials as they arrive (1)
- Providing templates to cut out materials (1)
- Having standard operating procedures at each process (1). **(2)**

3   Any *six* from:
- A quality system will assure that products should meet customer expectations (1), for example about the size of the bear or for safety (1).
- It will reduce issues at customer and returns (1), for example due to seams coming apart due to incorrect sizes (1).
- It will allow the early interception of problems in production (1), saving the cost of working on faulty products at later stages in production (1).
- It will help in reducing waste/scrap (1) and associated costs for rework or replacement materials (1).
- It will promote consistency of finished products (1).
- Conformity to industry standards and regulations (1), for example for meeting safety legislation on small parts/choking hazards or toxicity (1). **(6)**

Page 102

1   Any *four* from, for example: MRP software looks at all of the products the company must make (1) and calculates what parts and materials are needed (1) and when they are needed (1). The software outputs a list of the total quantity of

each different part or material to be ordered each week (1) and a detailed production schedule, showing what parts should be made on which processes (and when) (1). **(4)**

2. Putting together orders means materials can be delivered in bulk which may get discounts **(1)**.

3. Any *four* from, for example:
   - The software is expensive (1) and requires training to use (1).
   - The company must follow the schedule (even if it would be easier to make something else that is also needed) (1) otherwise they may run out of materials (1), stopping production (1).
   - The software depends on accurate data being input for demand and materials lists (1).
   - Sudden changes in demand can result in late orders (1). **(4)**

4. The company will make a variety of different parts or products (1). The quantity of each product may be different each week/month (due to customer orders) (1). **(2)**

Page 103

1. Inventory is the materials in stock, work-in-progress and finished goods that the company has (1).

2. JIT is an approach to manufacturing where components are ordered to arrive only when they are needed (1) and products are made as and when they are needed – not before they are needed (1). **(2)**

3. Any *eight* from, for example:
   Advantages
   - Less inventory (1) = less money invested or borrowed (1)
   - Less area needed for stores (1) = less cost of space (1)
   - Less 'double handling' (1) = less stores workers (1)
   - Overall reducing the amount of money invested in the business and the cost of production (1)

   Disadvantages
   - Risk of stopping production on their own line (1) or at the customer (1) due to late deliveries (1) or quality issues (1)
   - Difficult to respond to sudden changes in demand (1) and may miss opportunities where customers need immediate deliveries (1). **(8)**

Page 104

1. Lean manufacturing is concerned with reducing waste in manufacturing (1).

   Then, any *two* of the following points: as this will reduce costs (1), meaning either increased profits (1) or allowing customers to pay less (1). **(3)**

2. (a) Transportation waste is the unnecessary movement of materials (1) which requires labour time (1) and equipment resources (such as forklifts) (1) both of which incur costs (1). **(3)**

   (b) Inventory waste means materials that are not currently being processed (1) which is a waste, as companies have to invest money to buy the materials (1) which could be used for other purposes (1). **(3)**

   (c) Movement waste is wasted time or effort by workers (1) who are paid during this inefficient action (1) or could produce more products if the process was more efficient (1). **(2)**

   (d) Waiting is a waste where materials are not being processed whilst awaiting the next manufacturing operation (1). Similar to inventory, this is a waste as companies have to invest money to buy the materials (1) which could be used for other purposes (1). **(2)**

Page 105

1. (a) Over-processing is producing work that is higher quality than needed (1) or carrying out more work on a product than is needed (1) as work takes labour time, which must be paid for (1). **(3)**

Answers: Workbook

(b) Over-production means making more products than the customer needs (1) as excess products end up in stores as inventory (1). This is a waste as companies have to invest money to buy the materials (1) which could be used for other purposes (1). **(3)**

(c) Defects are products that fail to meet customer expectations or fail quality control checks (1) as it takes time to inspect for and fix defects (1) and therefore involves labour cost (1). **(3)**

2 For example, working to a tighter tolerance than required by a customer. **(1)**

3 For example, including apps on a mobile phone that the user does not require (1) as someone will have been paid to spend the time writing the app; or providing a high quality surface finish for visual appeal on a part that will be inside an engine (1); or making a product to a tolerance of ± 0.5 mm when the customer only needs it to be ± 2 mm (1). **(3)**

Page 106

1 Globalisation is a process where companies operate on an international scale (1). It typically involves centralising manufacturing in 'lower cost' countries (1) and shipping products around the world to markets in different countries (1). **(3)**

2 As products are made in only one location, they need to be transported to their end markets (1). This normally increases how much transportation is needed (1). For example, sports shoes might be made in India (1), then shipped to the UK and USA to be sold (1), rather than being made locally to where they are needed (1). [Award up to *four* marks for any suitable example]. **(4)**

3 Any *six* from: International standards describe the properties, safety needs and testing requirements for products (1) so the company will know what to make and how to check it meets the requirements (1).

If a product conforms to a standard, all users should have a clear understanding of what they are buying (1) and confidence that it will meet the stated expectations (1).

Without standards every country may have different requirements (1), meaning that the products may have to be made differently (1), reducing the benefits of manufacturing in quantity (1).

If companies can demonstrate that their product meets the standards it may also help them be allowed through customs/to access their different markets (1). **(6)**

Page 107

1 Any *two* from: There will be reduced employment opportunities for production workers in Great Britain, France and Germany (1) and increased opportunities for workers in China (1). They would still need workers in each country to order the products from China and to distribute the products (1). **(2)**

2 Any *four* from: The employment conditions would work to different laws (1) which could mean that there would be less consideration of the wellbeing of the workers making the products (1), with longer working hours (1), lower rates of pay (1), increased rates of accidents (1), and possible use of child labour (1) which would not be acceptable in the countries where the products were previously made (1). Customers may object to this, reducing sales (1). **(4)**

3 Any *four* from: By having one single factory making more products, the company may be able to use more automation (1), reducing the amount of labour (and therefore labour cost) per product (1). They may also be able to buy materials in larger quantities, getting discounts (1). The cost of labour in China may be a lot lower, meaning that the company could reduce their prices or make more profit (1). However, there would be additional transport costs to ship the products, which would reduce the cost savings (1). There may be redundancy costs to pay the existing workers, which would increase the product cost (1). **(4)**

Page 108

Up to 12 marks from:

Economic implications

- Reduced costs of manufacture may allow more profits or lower costs to the customer, which could increase sales (1)
- There may be opportunities for economies of scale (1) although to an extent these may not be fully achieved as the different sports teams will all require different shirts (1)
- May allow growth by the company, as it could start selling to customers in the region of the manufacturing site (1)
- Increased employment opportunities in India (1), offset by reduced employment opportunities in the European countries (1), which could reduce the amount of money locally available to buy the shirts (1)
- They might redistribute some wealth from the UK to India (1)
- Some customers might have preferences for products manufactured locally (1), which could lead to reduced sales (1)

Social and ethical implications

- There is the risk that child labour may be used (1)
- Health and safety regulations might not be as strict, increasing the risk of worker injuries (1)
- Customers might choose not to buy the product if it does not meet their ethical standards, reducing potential sales (1)

Environmental implications

- There might be more need for transportation, increasing the carbon footprint of the product (1) and contributing to global warming (1)
- There might be less environmental controls in India, leading to increased local pollution (1) and resultant potential effects on health (1). **(12)**

Acknowledgements

The authors and publishers acknowledge the following sources of copyright material and are grateful for the permissions granted. While every effort has been made, it has not always been possible to identify the sources of all the material used, or to trace all copyright holders. If any omissions are brought to our notice, we will be happy to include the appropriate acknowledgements on reprinting.

Thanks to Getty Images for permission to reproduce images

Cover Nitat Termmee/GI; *Inside* Youst/GI; Jamroen Jaiman/GI; Gmnicholas/GI; Dekiart/GI; Dex Image/GI; Westend61/GI; Jordan Lye/GI; Prapass Pulsub/GI; Westend61/GI; Martinns/GI; Ladislav Kubeš/GI; Atlantide Phototravel/GI; Carla Gottgens/Bloomberg/GI; Prasit Photo/GI; Technotr/GI; Abstract Aerial Art/GI; John P Kelly/GI; Heidijpix/GI; Monty Rakusen/GI; Kbwills/GI; Obradovic/GI; Mechanical fasteners - author's own image; Lovro77/GI; Monty Rakusen/GI; Maxbmx/GI; Chonticha Vatpongpee/GI; Liuhsihsiang/GI; Savushkin/GI; Waldo Swiegers/Bloomberg Creative/GI; Smith Collection/Gado/GI Shaun Roy/GI; Iantfoto/GI; Ambaradan/GI; Arand/GI; Oscar Porras González/GI; Peter Dazeley/GI; Toshifumi Kitamura/AFP/GI; Teekid/GI; Laurence Dutton/GI; Liuhsihsiang/GI; Phototalk/GI; Image Source/GI; Gilaxia/GI; Monty Rakusen/GI

Key: GI = Getty Images